W9-CLE-106

Ownership and Productivity
of
Marine Fishery Resources

Ownership and Productivity
of
Marine Fishery Resources

An Essay on the Resolution of Conflict in the Use of the Ocean Pastures

Elmer A Keen
Professor of Geography
San Diego State University

The McDonald and Woodward Publishing Company
Blacksburg, Virginia
1988

The McDonald and Woodward Publishing Company
P. O. Box 10308, Blacksburg, Virginia 24062-0308

Essays on a Changing Planet

Ownership and Productivity of Marine Fishery Resources
An Essay on the Resolution of Conflict in the Use of the Ocean Pastures

All rights reserved. First printing, 1988
Printed in the United States of America
by Lawhead Press, Inc., Athens, Ohio

95 94 93 92 91 90 89   10 9 8 7 6 5 4 3 2 1

Library of Congress Cataloging-in-Publication Data

Keen, Elmer A., 1926–
    Ownership and productivity of marine fishery resources.

    Bibliography: p.
    1. Fishery policy.   2. Fishery management, International.
3. Fishery resources.   I. Title.
SH328.K44   1988   333.95′6   88–794
ISBN 0-939923-05-X (pbk.)

Table of Contents

Acknowledgments

The central idea of this book, the need for full ownership of fishery resources, was developed in Japan in 1977 while I was researching the complex harvester rights that evolved over time in Japanese fisheries. Fishers, fishery administrators, and fishery scientists in Japan who helped me are far too numerous to mention by name. Collectively, I express special appreciation to personnel of the National Federation of Fisheries Cooperative Associations of Japan (Zengyoren) main office in Tokyo and of member cooperatives in Kanagawa, Nagasaki and Ehime prefectures; to fishery specialists in the fishery research laboratories of Kanagawa and Shizuoka prefectures; and to personnel of the Japanese Fisheries Agency central office and research laboratory in Tokyo. Individually and by name, I acknowledge a special debt to the late Professor Shoshichi Nomura of Yokohama National University, who aided me on a lengthy field excursion through southern Japan and numerous short trips to fishing ports in Kanagawa Prefecture, and to Professor Akira Hasegawa and his colleagues at Tokyo University of Fisheries who contributed ideas and sources of information too numerous to mention. And lastly among those in Japan, my debt to the late Dr. Hiroshi Oguri, Professor of Geography at Tokyo Gakugei University, is one that extends back to 1953 when he first introduced me to his special fields of research—common fishing grounds and common forests of Japan—and concludes only with his death in February 1988. It is to his memory that I dedicate this book.

My recognition of the poor basis that harvester rights provides for fishery resources management came through the help of colleagues in Japan. Fleshing out the seeds of ideas planted there, and presenting them in this book, has been helped immensely by numerous individuals in the United States and Canada. Those to whom I am greatly indebted include the late Professor W. R. Derrick Sewell and his colleagues at the University of Victoria in British Columbia who commented on an earlier version of this manuscript, and to personnel of the National Marine Fisheries Service office in Washington, D.C., who contributed to a collective letter of comments on the 1986 version that led to an extensive rewrite of the manuscript. Dr. David Fluharty, University of Washington, and Dr. Fred Olson, Global Ocean Consultants, Inc., reviewed this manuscript at the request of the publishers, and their comments also resulted in major improvements to this book. Among colleagues at my own institution, San Diego State University, I extend special thanks to Professors Virginia Flagg and Warren Johnson. Editorial comments of the publishers, Jerry McDonald and Susan Woodward, and my daughter, Carolyn, did much to straighten out murky presentations that readers can fully appreciate only by seeing the original manuscript. All of the above, and others, have contributed much to this book. Any errors of fact and interpretation are, of course, my responsibility.

Preface

The United States vigorously resisted claims made in 1950 by several Latin American countries to fishery resources within 200 nautical miles of their coasts. In 1976, however, the passage of the Fishery Conservation and Management Act in the United States unilaterally extended control by the United States over all but highly migratory fishery resources within a distance of 200 nautical miles from its coasts. Numerous other countries immediately followed suit. By the time delegates to the United Nations Law of the Sea Conference finished their work in 1982, the 200 mile concept had gained general acceptance. The new Law of the Sea Treaty, in effect, gave coastal countries ownership of all natural resources, mineral as well as biotic, located within 200 nautical miles of their coasts. The United States chose not to sign the new treaty, but in 1983, President Reagan issued an Executive Proclamation that matched rights claimed by the United States to rights permitted by the treaty.

The United States, because of its long coastlines and numerous island territories, gained a much larger area in this recent dividing up of the oceans than did any other country. Its Exclusive Economic Zone (EEZ), as these newly established marine natural resource areas are called, contains some of the world's most productive fishing grounds. The United States' EEZ also contains large quantities of mineral deposits that promise to be of great value. The United States is now the world's richest nation in fishery resources, and probably in ocean mineral resources.

The citizens of the United States have shown little interest in their newly acquired wealth. A lack of public interest or concern is of no great consequence as regards arrangements for management of the mineral resources. The institutional arrangements, that is, the customs and laws governing the use of the mineral resources, basically are sound. These arrangements recognize the full public ownership of all seabed minerals. While not perfect, they provide a framework under which the resources can be developed rationally and for the benefit of the citizens as a whole. For example, the oil fields of the continental shelf are managed in a full ownership framework by a public agency, leased under an auction bid system, and operated in a way designed to maximize benefits to society.

The same cannot be said of marine fishery resources. Fishery resources traditionally have been managed under a common property (open to harvest by everyone) framework that worked well when fish were plentiful. However, stocks of the more desirable species of fish are no longer plentiful; under common property ownership, they are almost certain to become even less so. Ownership that gives rights to fishery resources comparable to rights exercised by owners of agricultural, forest, range, and mineral resources is needed. Full ownership, as I herein call that form of ownership that gives such rights, provides incentives to look after a resource and increase its productivity. Common property ownership provides no such incentives. Natural resources that are open to use by everyone are looked after by no one.

Full ownership would bring an abrupt change in the rules of fishing that, not unexpectedly, leaves commercial fishers feeling nervous. Fishers resist change, and understandably so, unless they receive assurance that the change will improve their lot, or at least not affect it adversely. Fishery resource management specialists agree that full ownership provides by far the most effective framework by which to maximize benefits from the fishery resources. However, most management specialists support commercial fishers in their opposition to changing to this more effective framework.

Fishery management specialists cite a lack of interest on the part of the average citizen as the basic reason against changing to full ownership. Their reasoning is as follows. The decision to change the ownership arrangements would have to be made in the political arena. The benefits of changing ownership to voters who are not directly associated with fisheries are not large enough to make their involvement in the problem worth their time. Therefore, the fishing industry, and especially the fishers, will continue to make the rules for exploitation of fishery resources even though these rule are not in the best long-term interests of the public. The fishing industry is against full ownership. Working for full ownership is thus a waste of time because the industry will prevent passage of the necessary enabling legislation.

Citizens at large have shown a singular lack of interest in what happens to the rich marine fishery resources taken over in their name. I was in Japan in April 1977 when the United States' Fishery Conservation and Management Act went into effect. It made front page headlines in Japanese newspapers and was the subject of lengthy television programs commenting on its effects. The American news media gave it scant attention. News of President Reagan's proclamation of 10 March 1983 that extended United States' control over all marine resources to a distance of 200 miles rated the lower half of the left-hand column of page seven of The New York Times. The remaining seven columns of the page were devoted to an advertisement. An action that approached the Louisiana Purchase in importance to the United States received scant notice by the media, whereas the Louisiana Purchase received much attention in the media of the time. Could the difference rest in terms of acquisition? Does having paid for one and not the other help to explain the difference in media coverage?

Changes in public interests favorable to legislative change in the ownership of fishery resources have occurred in recent years. Fish has become a much more popular food. Marine recreational fishing has grown rapidly in popularity in recent years. The decreasing production of the more desirable species of fish has come to be of direct concern to a much larger segment of the population as a consequence. In a more general way, public interest in the oceans and all of its resources is growing. This interest is reflected in a growth in the size and number of organizations formed around aspects of the marine environment. Many of these organizations are taking a more active role in political processes relevant to changing arrangements for managing ocean resources.

A major purpose of this book is to develop further interest among all citizens of the United States, in whose name United States' control of its bordering oceans was extended to 200 miles seaward, in the management of marine fishery resources. The direct economic interests that all citizens have in these resources would, if fully understood by them, result in far more attention than that described above. Neither the media nor the public at large is very well informed as to the bases for these interests. In part, the lack of understanding results from the complexity of factors involved in the problem. The problem is complex, but not so complex as to be beyond the comprehension of anyone willing to spend a few hours reading and reflecting upon the essential factors. That more people are not informed results largely from the lack of good summary sources of information. Having rejected full ownership as a political impossibility despite recognition of its intrinsic merits, experts in the field of fisheries management have written nothing to define benefits that could accompany its adoption. Reams have been written for both specialists and laymen on ways to solve the problem of overfishing with harvester rights in a modified commons framework. Explanatory studies on full ownership, however, simply do not exist for either specialists or lay persons.

I am convinced that full ownership provides by far the most reasonable framework for management of marine fishery resources just as it does for most natural resources, whether terrestrial or marine. The reasons for this are not beyond the abilities of the non-specialist to comprehend; the potential benefits to everyone, fishers and non-fishers alike, are large enough to make it worthwhile for everyone to work toward the change. I have tried to write to inform citizens at large that they do have an interest in the ownership of marine fishery resources, and that they would benefit by taking steps to protect these interests. Specialists in fisheries management also may find this book worthwhile. The facts will be familiar, but the interpretations may convince that the rejection of full ownership merits rethinking. A management system based on full ownership can create far more benefits for everyone, fisher and non-fisher alike, than is afforded by present arrangements for harvest of fish. If the benefits that can come from full ownership are widely understood, then change to full ownership should come as a matter of rational development through our political processes.

1

"The Strange Productivity Curve"

This book is addressed to everyone who would like to see an increase in the abundance of fish. This includes those who would like to catch more fish but find fishery resources so depleted that going fishing is scarcely worthwhile. It includes those who would like to eat more fish but find the price has climbed beyond their reach. In short, it includes everyone who would like to see fish of the more highly valued species restored to, or possibly raised beyond, their former levels of abundance.

The price of different species of fish reflect their abundance and availability. Fish, as many of us remember, have not always ranked close to luxury foods in price. Many fish retailed for about the same price as chicken as recently as the mid-1960s; they now cost more, on average, than does beef. Corrected for inflation, the price of beef and pork has remained more or less unchanged since the mid-1960s, and the price of chicken has declined. The real price of fish, in contrast, has more than doubled and keeps on rising.

A question of fundamental interest to those of us who like fish is why fish prices increased so rapidly while those for red meats and chicken remained relatively stable or decreased. Fine tuning of the answer to this question would require attention to conventional aspects of economic analysis—to changes in technology, relative labor costs, methods of marketing, consumer preferences, and so forth. But conventional factors account for only a small part of the answer here. For most of the answer, we must turn to the law of supply which states that the higher the price of a commodity, the larger will be the quantity supplied.

The law of supply functions as expected for meat and poultry. As the demand for these items increases, prices rise; farmers react to the prospect for higher income by producing more animals and fowls. An

1

increase in demand also raises prices for fish, and fishers, too, are thus motivated to harvest more fish. However, when stocks of the desired fish become overexploited, as many have come to be, the result is fewer fish, not more.

Agreement is complete among fishery management experts as to why the law of supply works with agriculture but not with fisheries. Crops, cows, hogs, and chickens are owned in full throughout their life cycle. Increases in value of crops or animals because of growth in number or size or for any other reason accrue to the owner. The prospect of higher income thus inspires the owner to invest to produce more crops or animals in response to price increases, and to do so as efficiently as possible. The total supply of the product increases as a consequence, demand at the new price level is met, and production stabilizes at the higher level of supply.

An increase in price also motivates fishers to invest additional time and money in order to catch more fish and thus profit from the higher prices. As long as stocks are not overfished, an increase in price does lead to a larger harvest for the market. However, fish, except for those produced by aquaculturists (fish farmers), are not owned until they are captured. Therefore, no incentives exist for a fisher to invest to add to the total stock of fish since the additional fish produced would not belong to anyone until they were caught. Chances that the investor would catch enough of them to make the investment worthwhile are slim indeed. Because stocks of many desired species have come to be overexploited in recent years, investment in additional fishing effort on these stocks can only lead to further depletion and a decrease in total production of fish from them.

The law of supply seemingly goes into reverse with the overexploitation of a renewable resource that is unowned until harvested. Exploitation by commercial hunters of game birds and animals as the frontier of European settlement spread across America provides ample evidence of "reversal" of that law. Can different results be expected with unowned fishery resources? Fishers are, after all, hunters, not farmers.

Agreement is less than complete among fishery management specialists as to how to get fisheries back on course with the law of supply. The time tested way, ownership comparable to the ownership that gives incentives to the farmer, rancher, and forester to increase production when prices rise, has been rejected as too disruptive and probably politically impossible.[1] The most widely advocated alternative, limiting the number of fishers with rights to harvest, has not worked very well. The extra share of the pie received by recipients of these rights goes to improve ways to hunt fish produced by nature, not to help nature to produce more fish. Cursory study of the effects to date of such harvester rights leaves no question that this alternative can create more problems in the long run than it solves.

2

I am convinced that the time tested formula of full ownership[2] of the resource, as ownership comparable to that of the farmer, forester, and rancher is referred to in this book, has been rejected prematurely. Not only will full ownership work better than any form of harvester rights, it can also be implemented with little disruption and *no economic hardship to anyone* if issues concerning it are understood by the public at large (chapter 5). Once implemented, everyone will enjoy added economic benefits from marine fishery resources.

The reasons for converting marine resources to full ownership are identified in this introductory chapter. Reasons set forth without supporting evidence are at times difficult to accept, but the reader is urged to be tolerant at this stage. Supporting evidence for the conclusions that are presented in this chapter, while complex in totality, does, in a way, resemble a jigsaw puzzle. The ability to recognize individual pieces helps immensely in fitting them together; the total picture will become clear when the last piece falls into place. Supporting evidence for generalizations concerning individual pieces of the fisheries puzzle is presented in the following chapters. Readers who are familiar with the problems of managing natural resources will recognize many of the pieces, and may wish to skip certain sections and skim others. Those less familiar with such problems may find reading all chapters to be worthwhile.

My conviction of the need for full ownership of marine fishery resources is based on analysis of the nature of fishery resources and of the stage that we have reached in their exploitation. My conviction is complete. I am less than certain as to *where* ownership is best vested. My own leanings are toward public ownership at the national level, but I accept private ownership in a corporate framework as an alternative well worth exploring. My main goal here is to point out the considerable advantages that full ownership can bring. Once these advantages are widely understood and accepted, the place to assign ownership of the resource and under what conditions will evolve as a matter of national consensus.

The Tragedy of the Commons in Brief

The law of supply seemingly has gone into reverse for stocks of our more desirable fishery resources because (a) these resources are common property and (b) our use of them has entered what has been termed the tragedy of the commons.[3] In its purest sense, a common property resource is one that is open to use without restriction. Marine fishery resources remained as an almost pure common property resource until the end of the 19th century. Some nations did limit use of fishery resources within their territorial waters (within 12 miles or less of their coasts) to their own citizens, but the oceans beyond remained a true international commons open to fishing without reference to nationality. From early in this century, territorial waters came to be treated as a national commons by most countries with few restrictions on use by

3

their own citizens. The law of supply worked well under these arrangements as long as fish were plentiful. A few stocks in the North Sea and in the Atlantic Ocean off New England showed signs of depletion toward the end of the 19th century, and depleted stocks increased worldwide as demand for fish grew during the 20th century. As demand for species of the more desirable stocks exceeded the capacity of these stocks to produce fish, the law of supply went awry for those species.

The tragedy of the commons begins at the point where an increase in price causes supplies to decrease because of overexploitation. As supplies decrease, each fisher catches fewer fish but higher prices keep incomes at levels comparable to the time when stocks were harvested at levels below maximum sustainable yield (chapter 3). Decreased catches resulting from overexploitation may leave fishers as fishers no worse off than before; the rise in prices is often sufficient to support an increase in the number of fishers exploiting the diminishing resource. From the standpoint of the public at large, however, a mistake has been made. To continue to invest labor and capital resources in a fishing effort that results in fewer fish, when a change from common to full ownership provides incentives to invest in the natural resource itself and thus produce more fish, is a tragedy.

In prehistoric times when human populations were relatively low, natural resources were common property. Material wants could be met fully by harvesting nature's bounty; no need existed to control access to harvest of natural resources to prevent overexploitation of them. Ownership systems are troublesome to develop and even more troublesome to enforce. Ownership systems for natural resources were not necessary when human populations were small, and pressure on natural resources was light. As humans increased in numbers, the mere hunting and gathering of nature's bounty no longer met material wants. Investment of human effort to increase productivity became necessary; this in turn required control of access to harvest. For example, if everyone had the right to harvest the crops produced by a farmer, then the farmer would not invest the effort needed to produce the crops. The result was the ownership systems for terrestrial natural resources, and especially land itself, that we now take for granted.

The ownership change for resources of the land is complete for the most part. The increases in productivity of land in field, forest, and pasture that were made possible by full ownership staggers the imagination when we stop to think about it. Such change in ownership is necessary if we are to produce desired commodities in the quantities needed. This increased productivity involves investment of work and capital, the two factors of production amenable to increase through human effort, in the third factor, land, which is fixed in amount. As noted above, no one is likely to invest labor or capital to make land produce more if ownership comes only with harvest and everyone has the privilege of

4

freely participating in the harvest. If all of the land that is now in cultivation were still common property with the harvest of its products freely enjoyed by anyone, the total human population of the world would be only a small fraction of its present size.

Given the nature of the oceans, a change to full ownership is not likely to provide incentives sufficient to make them as productive as cultivated land. However, an increase in productivity at least comparable to that which took place on pasture and forest lands when they were converted to full ownership could reasonably be expected. The history of depletion of the forest and pasture resources in North America when they were open to harvest by all, and the subsequent recovery of these resources as they came under full ownership, suggests the benefits that the incentives of full ownership can provide for fishery resources.

The title of this chapter is taken from a graph, reproduced below as Figure 1, that was included in a briefing on the Fishery Conservation and Management Act of 1976 prepared by the National Marine Fisheries Service.[4] The graph uses stocks of fish at different levels of exploitation to show what happens as exploitation proceeds through the tragedy point for a common property resource. Fishing effort is measured on the horizontal axis, and catch is measured on the vertical axis. As can be seen, as long as stocks are less than fully exploited, an increase in the amount of fishing effort increases the size of the catch. However, fishing effort in excess of that needed to harvest the maximum sustainable yield (MSY), shown at the top of the yield curve, of a stock of fish results in overfishing and decreased yields. The point of MSY marks the onset of the tragedy of the commons, which I also refer to herein as the *tragedy point*. The cost of harvest per unit of fish increases as the tragedy point is approached. For this reason, and to assure ample brood stock for stock replenishment, a full owner wishing to maximize benefits from a particular stock of fish would stop harvesting at the point labelled optimum sustainable yield (OSY).

Information presented in Figure 1 is highly generalized and should not be interpreted as showing precise relations between catch and fishing effort for the different stocks of fish shown. The relative status of the fish stocks selected by the National Marine Fisheries Service to demonstrate their *strange productivity curve* is, however, correct for the late 1970s when the graph was made. The position of the stocks of the different species on the curve approximates the status of the stocks at the time. The yellowfin tuna stocks of the Eastern Pacific Ocean, shown as being exploited at the MSY level, were being managed by the Inter-American Tropical Tuna Commission through use of annual quotas. The estimated MSY of the tuna stocks for the year was announced at the beginning of each year, and became the quota for that year. Once the quota was taken, fishing was stopped. From the standpoint of the fishery, year round exploitation would have been more desirable. That the quota of tuna usually was taken by early in April suggests that the fleet was

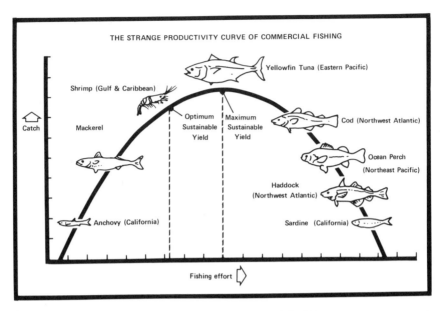

Figure 1. The relationship between fishing effort and catch for fishery resources managed under a common property framework. The status of stocks of eight species at different levels of exploitation is shown. The four stocks on the right hand side of the curve are overfished. See text for elaboration. (From the National Marine Fisheries Service, 1979.)

approximately three times the size needed to harvest the annual quota. As the tuna became more valuable and fishers of various nations joined the eastern tropical Pacific tuna fishery, pressures for a change in allocation of the quotas became unmanageable and, after 1980, the annual quota was ignored. Fortunately, the 200 mile EEZs implemented in the late 1970s have prevented severe overfishing of these tuna (Figure 2).

The stocks shown to the right of the tragedy point, or peak, on the yield curve were all overexploited at the time the graph was prepared. The cod and haddock stocks of the northwest Atlantic, traditional mainstays of New England and Atlantic Canada fishers, came under severe additional fishing pressure from European fishers beginning late in the 1950s. These stocks had joined the tragedy of the commons early in the 1970s. The ocean perch stock of the northeast Pacific was being lightly fished by American and Canadian fishers when Japanese and Russian fishers began to exploit them heavily in the mid-1960s. These stocks soon became overexploited. The strong reaction of New England and Pacific Coast fishers to this overfishing played a major role in the passage of the Fishery Conservation and Management Act of 1976. The California sardine stocks had been fished heavily before World War II; yields declined continuously after the War, and a moratorium was placed on exploiting these stocks in the 1960s. Reasons for the decline of the sardine stocks are still debated, but overfishing is generally accepted as a contributing cause. All of the depleted stocks shown on the graph have recovered somewhat since the Fishery Conservation and Management Act was implemented.

The three stocks to the left of the tragedy point were underfished— that is, they were able to support additional fishing pressure—when the graph was prepared. Subsequent increases in the price of shrimp moved the exploitation of the Gulf and Caribbean shrimp stocks closer to the MSY, but the natural history of shrimp is such that overexploitation of this resource is difficult. The shrimp harvest probably could be made with substantially less effort, but severe overfishing does not appear likely. The mackerel and anchovy stocks came under the protection of the Fishery Conservation and Management Act before overfishing occurred. Both stocks remain on the left side of the tragedy point although problems of coordinating management with Mexico have given some cause for concern about the California anchovy stocks.

Figure 2. A tuna purse seine vessel of the type developed for use in the eastern tropical Pacific Ocean. Among the largest fishing platforms in use today, these vessels average about 1,200 tons in hold capacity. (Figure courtesy Ken Raymond, Southwest Fisheries Center, National Marine Fisheries Service.)

The above brief description of the common property problem provides the essence of the causes of overfishing—which, in turn is the major problem in the management of marine fishery resources. The relationship between common ownership and the productivity of natural resources is discussed in detail in chapter 2. Problems associated with common property rights in fishery resources are elaborated upon with examples in chapter 3. Readers who remain dubious as to the benefits to be gained from full ownership as it exists for resources of the land, or who desire further explanation of the reasons for changing to full ownership, are invited to read those chapters. *The Strange Productivity Curve* does indeed seem strange when one is first introduced to it. By the end of chapter 3, however, most readers will no longer think of it as strange but as a logical consequence of depletion of a renewable common property resource. Let us now turn to a summary of the major benefits to be gained by moving out of the common property framework to one based on ownership comparable to that which exists for resources of the land.

The Benefits of Full Ownership in Brief

Harvest of fishery resources under a common property framework becomes increasingly wasteful once the tragedy point in resource exploitation is passed. Professor James Crutchfield of the University of Washington estimated that as much as four to five billion dollars were spent needlessly in harvest of North Atlantic fishery resources in 1980[5] (see chapter 5 for further details on estimates of waste). The commercial harvest of Pacific salmon resources of the United States could have been taken with only 10 percent of the effort expended in 1986 and with substantial improvement in both quality and quantity of landings. The landed value in that year was $494 million, most of which was eaten up by costs of harvest.[6] With the more rational fishing practices to be expected under full ownership, the value could easily have been raised to $600 million, of which at least 70 percent, or $420 million, could have been pure profit (chapter 5). The total value of all fish caught by United States fishers in 1986 approached three billion dollars of which at least one-third was wasted on excess fishing effort. This represents a potential economic rent (pure profit—see glossary) of one billion dollars, a figure that could be doubled easily in a few years under the more rational management and harvest practices possible under full ownership.

Fishery resources do not generate economic rent as long as they are common property. This is as it should be as long as the tragedy point is not passed. Since the natural stocks are not fully utilized, no investment is needed to help nature produce more fish to meet the demand for them. Any economic rent created would be diverted elsewhere, and total benefits to society from the fishery resource would decrease. Once the tragedy point is passed, however, everyone can be made better off economically if economic rent is collected and invested, at least as needed, to help nature produce more fish. This can be seen readily by reference to Figure 1.

8

To raise the price on the under-utilized Atlantic mackerel in order to create economic rent would raise the price of mackerel and reduce demand for it. The mackerel would be even further under-utilized. On the other side of the tragedy point, the excess effort wasted on the overfished species, the haddock for example, represents a loss of economic rent equal to the cost of the excess effort expended plus the value of fish not produced because of inadequate brood stock. Therefore, bringing the overfished haddock under full ownership could result immediately in economic rent equivalent to the costs expended on excess fishing effort. Economic rent would increase over time as stocks recovered from overfishing. A full owner probably would find the investment of part of the economic rent in research and development of ways to produce more haddock too profitable to resist. *The strange productivity curve* shown in Figure 1 would assume the shape we have come to expect when prices of products of a renewable resource rise.

Benefits from a change to full ownership will be large and widespread. Those among us who like fish will benefit most directly since we will get better quality fish at lower prices. All consumers, however, will benefit in regards to food prices as higher fish consumption will reduce demand for competing foods. At present, the costs of management of fishery resources are paid almost entirely from general tax funds. All taxpayers will benefit as fishery resources management becomes self-supporting and fisheries begin to pay into the general tax fund— directly if the fishery resources are in public ownership, indirectly through income taxes if the resources are privately owned—rather than being supported by taxes. Most countries, the United States included, now pay substantial subsidies in one form or another directly to fishers. These expenditures add to the problems of resources management while depleting the general funds of governments. Removal, or at least reduction, of these subsidies as the number of fishers decreases, will also benefit taxpayers.

The reduction of fishing effort that will accompany full ownership may seem threatening to the economic well-being of everyone who depends on the harvest of fish for their livelihood. Under harvester rights as implemented to date, a reduction of fishing effort is threatening. Fishers who lose their rights to harvest, even if compensated for vessels and other equipment that they can no longer use, get no compensation for loss of income formerly gained from fishing. Payment of compensation for such losses always is resisted if it has to come from tax revenues. Suppliers of vessels and fishing gear receive no compensation as their businesses become depressed by the decreased demand for their wares, and the sale of surplus gear sold by leaving the fishery. Fishers who secure saleable licenses to fish often make out well financially, but subsequent buyers of the licenses are back where fishers were before restricted licenses were granted. Fishers with licenses find themselves increasingly circumscribed by regulations as to where, how, and for what they can fish. These regulations will become increasingly complex as fish become more valuable, and license holders strive to gain a larger share of the annual quotas for fully exploited stocks.

The economic rent earned under full ownership can be more than adequate to assure that no one suffers reduced income because of the change in ownership. That everyone who received income from the resources under the common property regime can be fully compensated from these profits is self evident since all of this income was gained under the wasteful fishing of the commons. Elimination of wasted fishing effort will create substantial savings immediately. Better fishing practices will increase the total value of the harvest; rejuvenation of depleted stocks will restore the value that was lost because of the overfishing of them. In summary, economic rent resulting from more efficient and effective harvest and restoration of stocks should be adequate to compensate for all losses of income associated with reduced fishing effort. As the needs for compensation decrease over time and as productivity increases, economic rent should soon be adequate to cover management costs also.

Despite the gross over-investment in fishing that now exists, the actual reduction in total fishing effort may well be less than expected at first glance. Under common property incentives, all income associated with the harvest of fish depends entirely on the value of landings. This precludes removal of *weed* fish (see glossary). These fish may have some value for animal food or fertilizer, but if they must be sold at any price below the cost of landing them such fish will not be sought under a system of common property or harvester rights. If caught incidentally while fishing for other species, weed fish will be thrown away at sea. A full owner may find it advantageous to pay for removal of weed fish, even those that have no market value, that compete with, and thus reduce the production of, desirable species. Farmers often pay more for the removal of weed plants than for the harvest of their main crop. A full owner of fishery resources should find it worthwhile to do the same. Thus more fishers may be employed when both weeding and harvesting become worthwhile operations than are now employed in harvest alone. In addition, weed fish will be used if their value covers the cost of processing them. Both fishers and consumers will benefit directly from the harvest of these weed fish for such direct value as they do have, and indirectly from the larger numbers of more valuable fish produced as a result of reduced competition from weed fish.

Some commentators argue that fishers will become "mere hired hands" under full ownership and that the lifestyle of fishers will be demeaned as a consequence. A reasonable model for harvest arrangements under full ownership would be that for grain in the grain belt of North America (chapter 3). Here farming enterprises produce the grain;

independent harvesting enterprises do much of the harvesting. Harvester lifestyles are romantic enough to have been featured in motion pictures. The harvest enterprises perform the same function under the same relationship to the producer that fishers would perform for the owner of fishery resources. Under these arrangements, in many respects fishers would have more freedom in carrying out the harvest operations than they do under the restrictive regulations that exist now. As with grain harvesters, they will be paid for work performed under contract, not by market value of the product harvested.

The most able fishers, the "highliners," will still be rewarded in higher monetary income and in recognition of their abilities by their associates. Under common property frameworks, harvesters can, in the long run, earn no more than a fair return on their labor and capital (chapter 3). Fishers, therefore, will do at least as well under full ownership as they did when everyone had the right to fish as much as they wanted. Where systems of harvester rights have been instituted, fishers find themselves circumscribed by increasingly onerous gear and catch regulations as managers try to prevent annual quotas from being exceeded. Under full ownership, fewer regulations of such nature will be needed. As with monetary benefits, non-monetary or psychic benefits to fishers can be as great or greater under a full owner system than under the present system.

Fishers, understandably, do have the most cause for concern in any change of the magnitude that is essential if we are to gain the benefits that full ownership of fishery resources can produce. The profits that will come with full ownership, however, can be used to assure the fishers that they will be better off as fishers, consumers, and taxpayers under the new system. Fishers can and should be given ironclad guarantees that their incomes will not be reduced by the change to full ownership. Legislation for the change to full ownership can include a stipulation that the economic rent created under the new system be used to guarantee fishers who wish to retire lifetime pensions based on incomes they earned as fishers. As an occupational group, the average age of fishers is high. With this guarantee of income, the numbers retiring may be large enough for those who wish to continue fishing to do so as a full time occupation. Reduction of the strong competition to catch the fish before someone else does will make fishing a more pleasurable and safer occupation.

So much for the introductory summary of the main conclusions which are presented and discussed, with supporting evidence, in the remainder of the book. The opportunities that can come with full ownership of marine fishery resources are too good to pass up. I invite those not convinced at this point to read on.

1   H. Scott Gordon recognized the effectiveness of full ownership of overexploited fisheries in what can be considered the seminal article for modern fisheries economics. Few comprehensive works on fisheries economics fail to cite Gordon's article, which was titled "The Economic Theory of a Common-Property Resource: The Fishery," *Journal of Political Economy* 62 (April 1954), 124–142. James A. Crutchfield, recognized as the doyen of fishery economists in the memorial volume cited in note 2 below, accepts the efficacy of full ownership but states that ". . . other pressures would prevent the establishment of monopolies over fishery resources even where this was technically possible" (James A. Crutchfield, "Economic Objectives of Fishery Management," in James A. Crutchfield, ed., *The Fisheries: Problems in Resource Management*, Seattle: University of Washington Press, 1965:54). One of the major "technical" difficulties present at the time of Crutchfield's writing, the requirement that "monopolies" be established in an international framework, was removed by the recognition of national ownership of fishery resources within 200 nautical miles of national coastlines by the 1982 Law of the Sea Treaty. As is pointed out in chapter 4, establishment of the 200 mile EEZs greatly simplified the establishment of a full ownership framework for the management of marine fisheries.

2   *Full ownership* as used here means that the owner, whether a private individual or a public or private agency, has the power to exclude others from use of the resource in question. It infers essentially the same rights as are associated with the term *private property* in the United States and other market controlled economic systems. I chose to use the term *full ownership* because it encompasses the assignment of exclusionary rights to either public or private agencies. As discussed in chapter 4, assignment of such rights to either a public or private agency provides an adequate basis for the management of marine fishery resources. Use of either *public ownership* or *private ownership* at this stage thus seems premature. For an explanation of why exclusionary rights are essential, see John V. Krutilla, "Reflections on Man's Relation to Nature," pp. 1–24 in Edward Miles, Robert Pealy, and Robert Stokes, eds., *Natural Resources Economics and Policy Applications: Essays in Honor of James A. Crutchfield*, Seattle: University of Washington Press, 1986.

3   Garrett Hardin, "The Tragedy of the Commons," *Science* 162 (16 December 1968), 1243–1248.

4   Provided by the National Marine Fisheries Service in response to a personal request for materials for use in lectures concerning institutional arrangements for fisheries management in the United States that I presented in Japan in 1979.

5   James A. Crutchfield, "Marine Resources: The Economics of United States Ocean Policy," *American Economic Review* 69 (1979), 260–271 and James A. Crutchfield, "Marine Resources," pp. 39–53 in Susan Hanna, *et al.*, eds., *Exploring Conflicts in the Use of the Oceans Resources*, Corvallis: Oregon Sea Grant College Program, Oregon State University, 1980.

6   Data herein for United States fishery landings are from the National Marine Fisheries Service annual statistical volume, *Fisheries of the United States*, for the year cited unless otherwise noted.

2

Why Do the Fishery Commons Need Fixing?

Marine fishery resources are, with few exceptions, still managed as common property. EEZs have, it is true, taken about 95 percent of the world's fishery resources out of the international commons and brought them under national control. Management systems are easier to implement under national law than under international law, and most countries have reduced pressure on overfished stocks in their EEZs to some degree. This has been done, however, by measures that do not redirect the incentives associated with the harvest of common property. The income of fishers still depends on the value of fish they land; they understandably wish to take full advantage of their time and equipment in order to maximize the value of their landings. This means that the incentives to overfish and to fish wastefully, and the lack of incentive to invest to improve overall productivity of the resource, remain unchanged. The pressure to increase fishing effort continues to grow as the price of fish goes up. Regulations to control fishing effort must be strengthened, and thus will become more onerous to fishers, if yields are to be sustained.

Fishery resource managers charged with making rules and setting quotas in the expanded national commons find themselves faced on the one hand with pressure from fishers who want higher quotas in order to capitalize on their time and equipment, and on the other hand with pressure from scientific advisors who like a margin of safety in their recommendations on the maximum allowable catch for each year. Recent experience with a small stock of fish off the Pacific coast of the United States shows how rapidly the profit motive under common property can lead to overfishing. This case study reveals what the impact can be on management when annual quotas are set with less than perfect information about the resource and pressure from fishers who want larger harvests.

The Great Widow Rockfish Hunt of 1980–1982

The Great Widow Rockfish Hunt of 1980–1982 is the title of an article by Donald Gunderson of the University of Washington's School of Fisheries. The widow rockfish in question inhabit waters off the coasts of northern California, Oregon, and Washington. Small numbers of these fish, which attain a length of about 21 inches and weigh up to five pounds, have been caught by bottom trawl fishers since bottom trawling began in these waters many years ago. A fish of low market value, and at one time thought to be rather sparsely distributed in the ocean, widow rockfish were caught incidentally when fishing for other fish rather than being a major target species themselves.

In 1979, a skipper from Oregon discovered that widow rockfish concentrate in mid-water at night in large schools that can be caught easily with mid-water trawls. Phenomenal fishing resulted; catches averaged 31 tons per hour in the beginning. With catches this large, the harvesting of widow rockfish became profitable even at low ex-vessel prices. Landings leaped from 1,107 metric tons in 1978 to 28,419 tons in 1981 (Figure 3). Prices, which normally averaged about 20 cents a pound, dropped to as low as six cents in 1981.

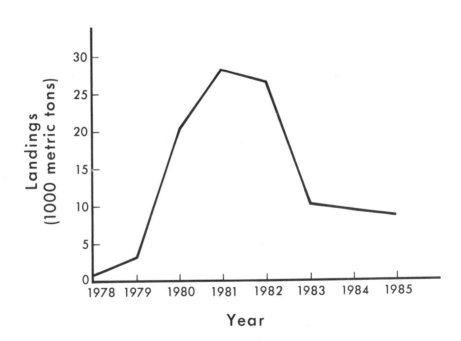

Figure 3. Widow rockfish landings during the "Great Widow Rockfish Hunt." (Data from *Pacific Fishing,* various issues.)

14

The skipper who discovered the schools, we can presume, held the information as close to his chest as possible, but the large catches inspired others to ferret out the information needed to join the harvest. Whereas only nine vessels delivered widow rockfish as a main catch in 1979, the number increased to 52 in 1980, and to 70 in 1981. The Pacific Fishery Management Council, the agency charged with management of these stocks, took action as the fear of overfishing emerged. The Council's Groundfish Team, which included marine scientists familiar with the widow rockfish resource, initially recommended a maximum catch of 18,300 tons for 1982. The team reduced its recommendation to 16,800 tons in July of that year after further study. Catches in 1980, the first full year that widow rockfish were a target species, and in 1981 exceeded the 1982 recommended catch by a considerable margin. This suggests that the widow rockfish had gone from an almost virgin state to being overfished in a little over two years, if the Groundfish Team's assessment of the maximum allowable catch was accurate.

The widow rockfish fishers, many of whom had purchased new vessels to enter the fishery, complained that a quota of only 16,800 tons would impose an unbearable economic burden on them after the large landings of 1980 and 1981. They pressured the Council for a higher quota. The Council members capitulated and adopted a 26,000 ton quota for 1982. The fishers caught the full quota plus 670 tons, but the yield per trip, an important measure of resource abundance, fell precipitously compared to what it had been in 1981 and 1982, and the individual fish caught were smaller. Everyone, fishers included, agreed that the widow rockfish resource was overfished by the end of 1982. The Council heeded its Groundfish Team's recommendation in 1983 and dropped the quota to 10,500 tons. It was dropped further in 1984 to 9,400 tons, and to only 7,400 tons in 1985. This was 40 percent of the estimated sustainable yield of 16,800 tons recommended by the Team in 1982. Had the Team's initial recommendation been followed, landings approximating the 1982 recommended quota presumably would have been possible for years to come. Gunderson wonders if the widow rockfish can recover in less than 20 years, the fishers regret their insistence on a high quota in 1982, and consumers are paying higher prices for fish than if the 1982 recommended quota had been followed.

Gunderson's purpose in writing this article was to use the widow rockfish as an example of what is happening to our fishery resources. To this end, he writes:

All of us are familiar with the plight of the American bison, a species that traveled in vast herds and dominated the prairie until their losing confrontation with European man and the Sharps rifle. However, few people are aware that a similar phenomenon is underway currently over our continental shelf. As with the bison, Pacific coast groundfish resources such as sablefish, rockfish, and sole are being harvested with little concern for long-term development. There is a lack of effective harvest control by government agencies, with the result that the wealth of these resources is slowly being squandered.

Can we blame the commercial fishers who depend on these resources for their livelihood? Theirs is a difficult life filled with danger, hard work, and sleepless nights. There are no guarantees that after their investments in vessel, fishing gear, fuel oil, and sheer hard work have been made they will be rewarded in appropriate measure. Indeed, the fish they seek are constantly schooling and dispersing, moving from fishing ground to fishing ground, and require a great deal of skill to locate and capture. Once the catch is in the hold the price they receive is subject to fluctuation and can vary widely over the course of the year, depending on the level of catches elsewhere in the United States, the level of foreign imports, freezer holdings from previous months, and even the price of domestic chicken. They depend on wild stocks of fish, the abundance of which is partially determined by environmental conditions that can change drastically from year to year. Is it any wonder, then, that commercial fishermen and the processors who buy their product take only the short-term view of stock conditions and economic conditions in planning their activities?[1]

Let us explore the question, "Can we blame the commercial fishers . . ." posed at the beginning of the preceding paragraph. We might feel sympathy for the fishers after reading Gunderson's thoughts concerning their hard work and sleepless nights. Agreement with the short-term view forced upon fishers and processors described at the end of the paragraph also comes easily. But where does the responsibility rest for the need for so many fishers to endure such a " . . . difficult life filled with danger, hard work, and sleepless nights?" Let us ask a few more questions.

Why did over 70 vessels enter the widow rockfish harvest when less than a dozen could easily have harvested the maximum allowable catch of about 16,000 tons annually? A fleet no larger than needed to harvest the annual optimum yield could have fished steadily throughout the year for years to come. Fish would have been more abundant; less time would have been spent looking for schools to catch. Prices of six cents a pound in 1980 and 1981 suggest that the market was flooded in those years, a direct consequence of excessive landings by fishers. While these low prices may have pleased consumers at the time, there can be no doubt that consumers would have enjoyed more rockfish at lower average prices in the long run if only as many vessels as needed had done the harvesting for them. One also suspects that the crews' daily life on those vessels would have been less difficult than when 70 or more vessels were competing with each other for a limited quota.

Turning to taxpayers, what happened after 1982 to the owners and crew of the excess vessels built specifically to harvest widow rockfish? Gunderson points out that the federal Fishing Vessel Obligation Guarantee Program of 1973 guaranteed up to 87.5 percent of the cost of vessel construction and that the Fishing Vessel Capital Construction Fund Program of 1970 allowed tax deferments for construction. The bills for the construction of new vessels for use in harvesting the widow rockfish resource are not likely to have been paid off in the three years that landings were high. Taxpayers subsidized overfishing—overfishing that was not in their interest as consumers—to the extent that fishers in question took advantage of the federally subsidized programs to build vessels that were not needed. Did taxpayers also pay unemployment benefits to some fishers after they had fished themselves out of a job? To the extent that the federal programs described were used, taxpayers ended up paying to create an erratic and decreasing quantity of fish that cost them both at the fish market and in their tax bills.

Fishers participated in the "Great Widow Rockfish Hunt" of their own free will. We must, therefore, assume the fishers' actions were rational from their standpoint, or at least so under existing institutional arrangements for harvest of the fish. But from the standpoint of the country as a whole, the severe depletion of the resource that resulted was disastrous, or, in the words of Garrett Hardin, a tragedy.[2] Why did it take place? Where does the blame for it rest?

The Tragedy of the Commons

The sequence of events described in *The Great Widow Rockfish Hunt of 1980–1982* has been repeated with increasing frequency in recent years. To fish more and produce less, when to fish less would produce more, is a tragedy. If the cause rests in everybody having the right to fish, why did it not happen earlier? Did fishers always spend more and more effort to catch fewer and fewer fish?

The answer rests primarily in the incentives under which a common property resource is harvested, and in the effects that the incentives have at different levels of exploitation. When a renewable natural resource is underutilized, an increase in price results in an increase in the flow of its products to consumers. The law of supply works as it should. Restricting rights to harvest the resource in order to reduce volume harvested would increase prices to consumers with no countering benefits.

Once demands on a natural resource exceeds nature's ability to produce it, however, a dramatic change takes place. An increase in price results in decreased production. If everyone continues to have the right to harvest the resource, the incentives, or perhaps more accurately, imperatives, of the commons result in decline of the resource to a point where it is no longer worth harvesting. Creation of rights that replace common property imperatives, on the other hand, set the stage for substantial increases in quantity and quality of production as demand grows.

The problems of overexploited common property can be, and often have been, stated in a few words. Most people involved with fishery resources management can roll them off without thinking. Students in my marine resources classes memorize and can repeat them, without faltering, forwards and backwards. But reasons why these problems exist seem to be put aside once working out ways to remove them is undertaken. Possibly because these problems can be so easily stated, the real reasons for their existence are not fully digested and made a permanent part of the mental matrix for solving the problems. Therefore, I provide below what may seem to be a far more lengthy explanation of the mechanics of these problems than the reader may think necessary. Those who so feel are invited to skip over this section, but I council them to keep in mind, and at the very forefront of their thinking, the tremendous damage the profit motive can cause once the tragedy point is passed. The widow rockfish fiasco provides a telling example; the explanation below illustrates the mechanics of the tragedy. It is cast in a simplified model of common pasture lands, the resource most often used to illustrate the problems of common property.

The Common Pasture Model

Pasture lands open to use by all, or at least open to enough people to illustrate the imperatives of the commons, are found in many countries today. They have existed in most other countries and often form a well known facet of their history. The battles between cattle ranchers, sheep ranchers, and squatters in the American West, all very much a part of its history and folklore, are a good example of the significance of control and use of range lands. The enclosure, that is, the establishment of full ownership in the sense used here, of common pastures in Great Britain played a much longer and even more conflict-ridden part in the history of that country than did the conflict over range lands in the United States. The British experience has been well studied and provides ample insight to illustrate thoroughly the imperatives of the commons.

Let us draw on the British experience to show why, in exploitation of a common property resource, production increases with demand until the tragedy point is reached and then decreases. The model used is hypothetical and simplified but fits the general record well. The time is about 1800, the place about 80 miles from London. The Industrial Revolution is gaining momentum; population and wealth are beginning to concentrate in London. Our resource in question is an upland area that has been recognized for centuries as a common pasture open to any and all for grazing their animals. To keep our model simple but still realistic let us assume the following about the pasture and its use.

- The carrying capacity of the pasture under natural conditions, that is, with no work done on it to improve its quality, is 100 dairy cows.
- The 25 farm households closest to it are the only ones using it. More distant households have the right to do so but, at the time, have ample pasture closer to home.
- Each household keeps two cows on the pasture. These are kept to assure dairy products for home use year-round. Milk in excess of home needs is used to make butter and cheese for sale, but the market is small and prices are low. Total benefits from each cow is equivalent to $100 annually.
- The farm population of the area remains constant since urban employment draws all youth to the cities except for one offspring and spouse who inherit the family farm.

Under the above conditions, all is well. Each of the 25 families receives $100 worth of benefits from the pasture at no cost other than driving the cows to and fro between it and home. Annual benefits from the pasture total $5,000 (50 cows at $100 each).

London grows and so does its market for butter and cheese. Prices rise to a level that supports transport of the butter and cheese to London by horse and wagon. Each cow's output comes to be worth $120 a year, enough to encourage each household to add another cow. Benefits from the pasture to each family climbs to $360, and total benefits to $9,000. Only three-fourths of the pasture's carrying capacity is used so the additional burden creates no problem. The market continues to expand, benefits from each cow rise to $125, each household adds another cow and now receives $500 in benefits annually free of costs other than driving the cows to and fro; total value is $12,500, and the pasture is fully utilized. No problem of overgrazing exists, but the addition of one more cow will create one.

Now let us assume that a railroad reaches the area, and that even raw milk can now be sent to London profitably. The value of production of each cow jumps to $200. The total gross value from the pasture reaches $20,000 at its capacity level of 100 cows. The profit motive provides the incentive to increase dairy herds substantially. Not only the original 25 households, but others at greater distances now find it worthwhile to drive their cattle to our common pasture. However, additional pressure without improvements, such as removing inedible plants or adding fertilizers, to make the pasture produce more forage will lead to overgrazing and a decrease in carrying capacity. For ease of computation, let us assume that for each cow added to the pasture in excess of 100, carrying capacity will be reduced by one cow—the 101st cow decreases carrying capacity to 99 cows, the 102nd to 98, and so forth. What will happen?

The tragedy of the commons sets in. The 101st cow decreases gross value produced by the pasture by $200 to a total of $19,800; the value of each cow's production from grazing on the commons falls, with slight rounding, to $196. The added cow thus decreases the value gained from the commons for all cows by $4 each, but nets the farmer who added it $196 less the cost of driving it to the pasture for grazing and home again for milking. The economics of this to individual farmers is self-evident— cows keep getting added until the benefits from use of the commons equals the cost of driving the cows to it and home again. If 50 more cows than the pasture can carry are added, the total annual value of production will drop to one-half or $10,000, and the value of production per cow to $40. Anyone who can drive cows to and from the pasture all year for $40 or less will continue to add cows.

The pasture is now severely depleted. The reduction in production of milk, butter, and cheese is a tragedy to all—to the farm families, to consumers in London, to citizens of the country as a whole. Is it any wonder that the phrase "as barren as a commons" appears frequently in British literature of the period? Similarities between the examples of the English commons and the widow rockfish are not coincidental. The imperatives of the commons work implacably whether on land or in the ocean.

The above example demonstrates one of the more frequently cited imperatives of common property—*harvest the resource before someone else does*. This means that each harvester continues to harvest until the resource is depleted. The model shows the same destructive imperatives that exploitation of the widow rock fish showed once maximum sustainable yield was exceeded. The profit motive served well before; it rapidly brought disaster afterward.

A second aspect of the tragedy, the common property imperative *to forego investment that would improve productivity of the resource*, gets less attention but is, in its end effect, equally tragic. To illustrate, let us assume that $10 worth of labor to remove inedible plants or $10 worth of fertilizer would increase the carrying capacity of our common pasture by one cow. At $200 annually per cow, this $10 yields a 2,000 percent return, a return no full owner would be so foolish as to pass up. A balanced mix of all investment options available—fertilizing, weeding, introduction of more nutritious plants, and the like—to improve the pasture probably would double the carrying capacity of the pasture before the cost of feeding the last cow equalled benefits from doing so. If a growing market forced prices up, capacity would be improved proportionately by additional investment.

Returns of 2,000 percent may seem ludicrous at first, but the first investments in a resource after the tragedy point is reached can pay off at phenomenal levels. The cost of clearing salmon streams to improve spawning habitat, for example, has paid off at a higher rate than in the example used above. But would users, either individually or collectively, make this investment in a common property resource? A 2,000 percent return would seem, at first glance, to be incentive enough to get at least one extra cow fed. Not so if individuals act rationally from the economic viewpoint.

An individual investing in our common pasture as described would lose money on the investment. Value added by $10 would yield $200 annually but this added value would be shared by 101 cows. The return to the investor on an extra cow thus would be $2.00 for a loss of $8; if he owned 5 of the 101 cows, he would just break even. A much more rational course is to invest enough in one's own land to grow feed to supplement the cow's needs not met by grazing on the commons. The return on investment on one's own land would never reach anything like 2,000 percent if only because production of other valuable crops would be given up, but the return would all go to the investor.

Would it be worthwhile for all who put cows on the pasture to work together to increase the productivity of the pasture beyond its natural level? Hardly. Since anyone and everyone has the right to use the pasture, improvement by collective action of current users would only make it worthwhile for farmers who live at a greater distance to drive their cattle to the pasture. This would be a never ending process. Even if all newcomers joined in, the costs of getting all users to cooperate would grow to irrational proportions. As before, farmers would be better off to invest in their own land to produce forage to supplement that of the common pasture than to invest in the common pasture itself.

Another imperative of importance in understanding the harvest of ocean pastures, *take the best first*, can lead to considerable waste during the harvest. It was not brought out in the British common pasture model but is inherent in it. So far we have looked at the problem only from the standpoint of incentives provided to the entrepreneur, in this case the farmer. In the common pasture example, we logically think of the pasture itself, or more specifically, the plants in it that cows will eat, as the natural resource. The farmers' cows do the harvesting. For fisheries, fish worth keeping become the natural resource of concern even though the ecological role of the fish and the cow are essentially parallel. The fishers harvest the fish and, in this sense, parallel the role of the cow. They also parallel the farmer in the entrepreneurial role.

The point to focus on here is the imperative to harvest the best first from the ecosystem. The cows, as one would expect, eat the most palatable plants first. As an ecologist would point out, these plants are there because they have been able to compete with other plants in the ecosystem. Selective grazing of the more palatable plants by the cows, however, gives the competitive edge to less palatable plants, and, as selective grazing further weakens these in competition with inedible plants, the pasture eventually is taken over by plants with no forage value. The total volume of vegetation produced may still be high, but the economic value of the pasture has become nil. Taking the best (most palatable) first, the second best when the best is gone, and on down the line means that the cows work to their own detriment when too many graze the pasture continuously. Would not selective harvesting have a similar impact on the ocean ecosystem?

The parallel of the fishers and the cows approaches perfection in one respect; the imperative to take the best (most valuable) first is difficult to resist. From the fisher's standpoint, it is as irrational to take the less valuable fish before the more valuable as eating the less palatable vegetation first would be from a cow's standpoint. We can assume the ecological impact of selective harvest is the same although it is far more difficult to measure because of the more complex ocean ecosystem. In one important aspect, however, there is a difference. When a cow unintentionally bites off (harvests) a less palatable plant while grazing on the more palatable ones, chances are she will go ahead and eat it. If fishing for the most valuable species is good, the fisher who catches a less valuable fish may throw it overboard even though the value of the fish would more than cover the costs of landing and marketing it. In this case, fish returned to the water are wasted if they die. Returning live weed fish to the ocean, on the other hand, increases the degrading effect of selective fishing on the fishery resources if the fish live.

The Salmon Example

Students in a marine resources class that I taught at the University of Victoria in British Columbia first brought the waste in fisheries caused by the *take the best first imperative* to my attention. I had pointed out that tropical fishery resources were less profitable to fishers than those of middle and high latitudes because the great variety of species from tropical waters made marketing more difficult. This leads to many fish being thrown away at sea. A student familiar with Victoria's salmon troll fishery, but presumably no better educated than I was at the time in the intricacies of commercial salmon fishing, pointed out that local salmon trollers also caught at least three species of salmon and wondered if any of these were wasted for the same reason. I answered that I thought not since all three were valuable and had a good local market. A student who fished during the summer spoke up, and, rather sheepishly I thought, said that this was not always the case. His explanation, made from the standpoint of the fishers, was as follows.

He and another student had signed on as crew the previous summer with an owner-operated salmon troller that fished off the west coast of Vancouver Island. The fishing grounds ranged up to a full day's run in distance from Victoria. The students helped to pay for food, bait, and fuel used on each trip, and were paid for their work on a share basis. Thus both crew and the skipper/owner of the boat wanted to maximize income from the trip. The boat could stay out for four or five days depending on how much time was spent trolling. They caught all three species of salmon—pinks, silvers and chinooks—taken by trollers. Chinooks over 15 pounds were the most desirable, being at the time worth almost twice as much as smaller chinooks and silvers, which were in turn worth a little more than twice as much as pinks.

As the student explained, if the fishing was too poor to fill the boat before supplies, especially fuel, ran low, all salmon caught were brought back to market. If fishing was good and the boat filled before supplies ran out, a different procedure was followed. Fishing continued; all pinks caught were thrown back, all silvers and chinooks were retained, and their weight equivalent in previously caught pinks thrown overboard. This continued until supplies ran low and the long trip back home could no longer be postponed. He did not recall how many fish had been thrown away on trips when fishing was good, but we inferred that under certain conditions and mixes of species, more could be wasted than were brought to market.

The student's story led me, after leaving Victoria, to calculate how much waste realistically could take place. I used the mix of catch that was taken during the week of 20–26 August 1979 in a management area off the coast of Washington for my calculation. The mix of the catch that week was 54 percent pinks, 40 percent silvers, and six percent chinooks. The average price per pound to fishers during August was $.75 for pinks, $2.30 for silvers, and $2.70 for chinooks. I assumed a five day trip of which three would be spent fishing, a boat of 10 tons capacity, and a catch rate that filled the boat in a day and a half. Given these conditions, I calculated that an extra day and a half spent fishing raised the value of my hypothetical fisher's landings from $29,000 to $44,000, and resulted in disposal at sea of 9.9 tons of pink salmon.

Given the condition of salmon stocks in 1979, such waste was unlikely—the high value of salmon had so many boats chasing so few fish that a full load of salmon of any kind probably would have made the newspapers. However, the Washington legislature subsequently imposed a moratorium on new salmon vessels and planned to reduce the size of the existing fleet through attrition. If the number of vessels drops sufficiently, or if hatchery programs underway raise the number of fish, my example could become frequent reality. The imperative under the commons to maximize income by taking the best first is indeed a strong one, and one not easily denied.

To summarize a somewhat lengthy lesson in the mechanics of the tragedy of the commons, three reasons stand out for change from a commons to a full owner framework once the tragedy point is reached. They are:

1. The imperative to exploit the resource before someone else does.
2. The imperative to take the most valuable species first.
3. The imperative to forego investment that would improve productivity of the resource.

As we have seen, these imperatives are powerful indeed and serve to degrade the resource once production no longer can be increased by increasing efforts to harvest alone. Full ownership removes these imperatives and replaces them with incentives to look after the resource in the same sense that farmers look after their land and the crops produced on it.

The Tragedy Point and Marine Fishery Resources

The tragedy point for marine fishery resources arrived much later than for most plant and animal resources of the land. Whether national rights should be established for the oceans did become a major issue among European powers after Pope Alexander VI divided the world oceans between Portugal and Spain in 1493. While fishery resources were not an issue that led to this division, the relevance of ownership of fishery resources to productivity did arise in the discussion pro and con in the century following but was rejected as irrelevant. Thus we find Hugo Grotius, the Dutch lawyer, whose book *Freedom of the Seas* strongly influenced the decision for narrow territorial seas, writing in the early 1600s:

> But why, it is asked, does the secondary law of nations which brings about this separation when we consider lands and rivers cease to operate in the same way when we consider the sea. I reply, because in the former case it is expedient and necessary. For everyone admits that if a great many persons hunt on the land or fish in a river, the forest is easily exhausted of wild animals and the river of fish, but *such a contingency is impossible in the case of the sea* (emphasis added).[3]

The separation to which Grotius refers was the removal of animals of the forest and fishes of the rivers from the "ancient community of rights," as he called common property, that permitted anyone to harvest them. To do so was "expedient and necessary" to prevent depletion of the animals and freshwater fish to a point of uselessness to anyone, a decimation Grotius believed impossible for marine fishery resources, given their abundance. Grotius' arguments carried the day, and freedom to exploit fishery resources of the oceans prevailed well into this century. If he were alive today, he would surely argue just as cogently to remove marine fish from his ancient community of rights.

Grotius' statement on resources rested on an objective assessment of conditions of his time. The game animal populations of European forests had been decimated severely, the fish of rivers sorely depleted. Property rights had developed because rights were expedient and necessary for continued productivity of these resources. Fishery resources of the sea, on the other hand, remained in a relatively prime condition well short of the tragedy point of exploitation. Fish from the sea were ample for all; the appearance of the adverse imperatives inherent in common

24

property resources was far in the future. Society was better off if resources of the sea remained open to uncontrolled use by everyone.

Nature's bounty from the oceans remained adequate for almost three centuries after Grotius wrote *Freedom of the Seas*. Overfishing of a few stocks of the North Sea did become a subject of concern in the latter part of the 19th century. This led to establishment in 1882 of the European Fisheries Convention, the first major international body established to deal with fishery resource problems. Halibut catches off New England began to decline at about the same time. The tragedy point was passed for a few more stocks of valuable species between the two world wars. Foremost among these were the halibut and salmon stocks of the northeast Pacific. The United States and Canada responded with conservation treaties for each. But for most of the world's fishery resources, Grotius' conclusions held true through the first half of this century. Fishery scientists at a United Nations conference on conservation and utilization of marine fishery resources held in 1949 concluded that the only overfished stocks were those of high value species in the North Atlantic and North Pacific, particulary plaice, halibut, and salmon. They produced a map showing 30 major stocks of commercially important species that were considered virgin or underfished. Ocean fishery resources as a whole produced fish in quantities ample to prevent any real pressure to remove fishery resources from the international commons through the 1950s.

The situation began to change late in the 1950s as major fishing nations expanded their fishing fleets and extended operations to all of the world oceans. The FAO annual report of fisheries statistics shows that the world landings of marine fish in 1950 was 18.7 million tons, the record to that time. The volume of world landings increased rapidly into the 1960s as virgin grounds of desirable species were opened up, and reached 56.5 million tons in 1968. Landings fluctuated over the next five years as the Peruvian anchovy fishery collapsed, and in 1973, stood at only one half million tons above 1968. Since 1973, landings have fluctuated while moving generally upward although at a lower rate than during the late 1950s and 1960s.

Increases in landings since the mid-1960s have come largely from stocks of previously unfished species and from industrial fish. Of the more valuable traditional species of finfish, only the tropical tunas have continued to show an upward trend in total landings. A few new species gained popularity, the orange roughy of New Zealand being an example that is well known in supermarkets of the United States, but landings of most other favorite food fish have declined. FAO statistics show that between 1970 and 1979, landings of Atlantic cod fell from 1.32 million tons to 1.15 million, haddock from 910,000 to 240,000 tons, and flounders from 1.32 to 1.15 million tons. The decline in landings coupled with a growth in demand has caused a sharp rise in price of these species.

Fish Prices Beyond the Tragedy Point

Fish now rank in price with the most expensive cuts of red meat available at the meat counter. An advertisement in October, 1985, for a San Diego supermarket, for example, listed halibut steaks at $3.99 a pound, exactly the same price as for filet mignon, their most expensive steak. The cheapest fish advertised was turbot at $1.98 a pound. Chicken was $.47 a pound.

Fish did not rank with beef in price before the supplies of favorite species began to decline in the late 1960s. Prices advertised in San Diego newspapers in October, 1960, had filet mignon selling at $1.98 a pound, halibut steak at $.59, rockfish filet at $.39, and chicken at $.33. Fish has moved from an inexpensive food ranking with chicken in price, to a luxury food ranking with the more expensive cuts of beef. In the 1985 advertisements, the cheapest fish exceeded the cheapest cut of beef in price by a substantial margin. In 1960, halibut could be bought at prices lower than most cuts of beef. Inflation pushed up the list price of all meats over the period, but fish rose much faster in real cost to the consumer as is shown in the supermarket advertisements.

Data from the *United States Statistical Abstract* give a more precise measure of the change, or at least one that is more representative of the country as a whole, than do advertisements in San Diego newspapers. The average prices received over the period by producers of different kinds of meat are shown in Figure 4. Producer prices, that is, prices received by the farmer or fishers, give a more accurate picture of changed relationships between the different items than do retail prices since producer prices do not include the costs of processing and marketing. As the graph shows, the price fishers received for the two traditional New England table fish shown rose far more rapidly after 1965 than did the prices of beef or chicken. In 1965, the price of both fish was about one-half that of beef and the same as that for chicken. By 1985, the price of both fish exceeded that for beef and was several times that for chicken. The rise after 1965 reflects the exploitation beyond the common property tragedy point of increasing numbers of stocks of fish.

An index of producer prices prepared by the United States Bureau of Labor Statistics provides yet another measure of the disparate rate of increase in price of fish compared to other meat items. The current producer price index is based on 1967 prices, a year close to the time fish prices began to rise precipitously. The average index of prices to producers for 1985, the last year for which data were available at the time of writing, showed finfish at 576 (1967 prices = 100), cattle at 228, hogs at 205, and young chickens at 209. Finfish prices thus increased over twice as much as did prices for beef, pork, and chicken.

Demand increased for all of the products discussed above in response to growth in population and incomes. Farmers increased production of beef, pork, and chicken in response to this growth in demand;

26

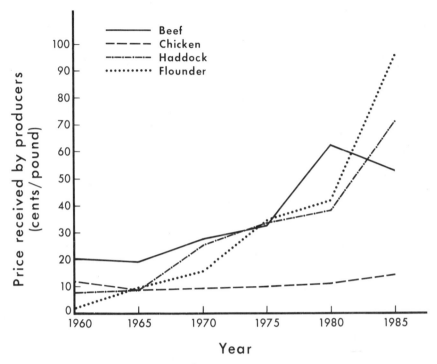

Figure 4. Trends in prices New England fishers received for haddock and flounder compared to prices farmers received for beef and poultry, 1960–85. Note the steady rise in the ex-vessel price of the fish species after 1965. (Data from *United States Statistical Abstract*.)

prices remained fairly stable in real terms as a result. Fishers also increased their investment to harvest fish but, alas, the result was fewer instead of more of the fish that consumers wanted. The resulting disparity of demand over supply forced prices for fish up much faster than the rate of inflation, and, under the imperatives of the commons, led to overfishing and lower production.

Most of the difference in the performance of fishers as compared to farmers rests in the common property nature of fishery resources. Farmers overproduced in most years in response to market demand and subsidies from the federal government. The profit motive gave the right signals, and, with subsidies, overproduction resulted. Demand for fish and subsidies to fishers also stimulated fishers to increase their incomes but produced the opposite result on total production. Fishing effort increased, but production of the more desirable species decreased. Overproduction in agriculture is a serious problem, but a relatively happy one compared to the decreasing productivity of fishery resources.

Must the price of fish continue to rise? A major reason that chicken is one of our cheapest meats is because of the high fertility rate of chickens. One hen can produce over 200 eggs a year; a cow can produce only one calf. Brood stock accounts for a much larger share of the cost of producing cattle than for producing chickens. The more popular food fish lay 5,000 to a million or more eggs a year. Would a full owner of the ocean pastures perhaps take advantage of the high fertility rate and bring the price of fish back down toward, or below, that of chicken? One who harvests fish under common tenure, as we have seen, lacks incentives to do so. Japanese salmon hatcheries have shown a benefit:cost ratio of six to one—a 600 percent return on investment. This suggests that the financial incentive to invest in salmon hatcheries is far more than ample if the returns from the investment can be channeled to the investor.

The Widow Rockfish Revisited

Had the nighttime concentrations of widow rockfish been discovered 15 years earlier, the rate of their exploitation would have been much lower. Fish of comparable value were plentiful; fishing them under the commons still would have made sense. By 1979, such fish were no longer plentiful. The fishers fell on the newly discovered schools of widow rockfish like a pack of starved wolves. Landings from them formed a short-lived blip in the fishery statistics of the Pacific coast states of the United States. The stocks of widow rockfish can, of course, be rebuilt to sustain an annual level of production probably twice the 7,400 ton quota set by the Pacific Fisheries Management Council for 1985. They will not be rebuilt, however, through voluntary restraints on harvest as long as fishers remain under the imperatives of the commons.

"Can we blame the commercial fishers who depend on these resources for their livelihood?," to pose again Gunderson's question presented above. Should we wonder that the commercial fishers take only the short-term view of the condition of stocks of species worth harvesting? Not as long as they continue to operate in a commons framework. Gunderson tells us that 70 vessels were engaged full-time in fishing in 1982 to land 27,000 tons, half again more than the recommended catch for that year. At the 50 tons per trip rates of catch common in 1980, with one trip each week, one vessel could harvest 2,600 tons a year. Eleven vessels could have harvested the entire 27,000 tons taken by the 70 vessels in 1982. Seven vessels could have harvested the estimated maximum allowable catch of 16,800 tons recommended in that year.

"Theirs is a difficult life filled with danger, hard work, and sleepless nights," Gunderson tells us of the fishers. Again, it is hard not to feel sympathy for fishers or to appreciate the risks that they take on the consumers' behalf. But need so many suffer so much to harvest the fish we consume? The imperatives of the commons are causing many more people than necessary to suffer the hard life of the fisher; overfishing and lower production result. All citizens, fishers included, suffer as taxpayers and consumers. Is it not past time to remove the imperatives of the commons by moving out of the common property framework?

1   Donald R. Gunderson, "The Great Widow Rockfish Hunt of 1980–1982," *North American Journal of Fisheries Management* 4 (1984):465.

2   Hardin, *op. cit.*, chapter 1, note 3.

3   Hugo Grotius, *Freedom of the Seas*, New York: Oxford University Press, 1916:57 (translated by Ralph Deman Magoffin).

3

Why Too Much Effort and How To Limit It

Excessive exploitation of a natural resource under a common property framework is as certain as death and taxes once the resource begins to run short. The imperatives of the commons assure this. These imperatives are powerful, as history has demonstrated time and again, and—in the case of biotic resources—can lead to extinction of valuable species.

A telling example of the tragedy of species extinction is the "penguin of the north," the great auk, that was slaughtered rapaciously for food from Iceland to Newfoundland as late as 1800. As great auks became rare early in the 1800s, museum directors began to offer fabulous sums for mountable corpses or eggs of the great auk. Hunters killed the last two known to be alive in 1844 for an Icelandic bird collector. The hunters would have appeared foolish had they not taken the two birds since someone else would have done so given the high value placed on great auks at the time.

Such are the imperatives of the commons. We would all be richer had someone established full ownership of the great auk, one of the few sea birds whose flesh humans have found to be palatable. Steller's sea cow, a creature with reputedly tasty flesh that grazed on seaweed around islands of the North Pacific and Bering Sea, is an equally tragic example from among the marine mammals. Fur seal hunters killed great numbers of these docile animals for use as food while hunting fur seals. The fur seals escaped extinction, but the last Steller's sea cow seen alive was killed by Russian hunters in 1768.

Fish, living as they do in a different element beyond the usual vision of humans, are not as easily captured as the flightless great auk or marine mammals and, to our knowledge, no marine fish species has become extinct because of overfishing. In fishery management circles, it is generally thought that fishing to extinction is next to impossible because the cost of capture rises precipitously as a species become scarce. However, a few, including the salmon and halibut of the northwest Atlantic, have become scarce. The latter is hardly worth fishing for anymore as a target species, but a few are caught while fishing for other species. The history of use and management of giant halibut in both the Atlantic and Pacific oceans provides a much broader perspective on the problems of fisheries management under a commons framework than does the widow rockfish discussed in the previous chapter. A brief look at the history of the halibut fishery can help clarify problems associated with management of fishery resources in a common property framework.

The Halibut Story

That abundance breeds contempt could be said of the Atlantic halibut in the first centuries of European settlement of New England. One author wrote in 1634 that "there are plenty of better fish that make the halibut of little esteem, except for the head which stewed is very good."[1] Another author writing in the 1880s said halibut "were as abundant in Massachusetts Bay at the turn of the century (1800) as to be considered troublesome pests as dogfish are at present."[2] New Englanders who relish the taste of local halibut must sorely regret the loss of such abundance.

The still abundant halibut had become a favorite food fish by the 1830s (Figure 5). The market was easily supplied. One boat returned with 15,000 pounds of fish after two days of fishing in March 1837; four men who went fishing from Marblehead in June of that year returned with 400 halibut in two days. But this good fishing was not to remain. Market demand grew; Massachusetts Bay and nearshore waters were soon fished out. By 1880, most halibut came from Grand Banks and other open ocean sites off New England. By 1900, fishers no longer found it worthwhile to target on halibut, although some halibut continue to be caught incidentally while fishing for the more plentiful haddock, cod, and other species of the ocean floor.

On the opposite side of the continent, another stock of halibut stood ready to fill the market gap created by the near demise of their Atlantic cousins. Slightly different biologically, little distinction was made between the two by consumers. Recently completed railroads to the Puget Sound area provided a suitable, if expensive, means of transport to eastern markets. As fishing grounds off the coasts of Oregon, Washington, and southern British Columbia became depleted, the extension of Canadian railways to Prince Ruppert improved access to market for halibut from northern British Columbian and southern Alaskan waters. Landings of Pacific halibut of 733 tons were recorded for the United States and Canada in 1888; landings grew steadily to 34,378 tons in 1915 after which they declined rapidly. The decline in landings resulted from

THE FRESH HALIBUT FISHERY.

THE FRESH HALIBUT FISHERY.

Figure 5. Longlining for halibut off New England (top) and unloading halibut at a New England port (bottom) when halibut were plentiful in waters off New England. The halibut stocks here were sorely depleted by late in the 1800s. (From Goode, *op. cit.*, note 2, chapter 3.)

33

a shortage of fish, not a fall in price. The rapidity with which the tragedy point was reached fell short of that for the widow rockfish discussed earlier, but must have been the record for a major stock of marine fish to that date.

The fishery followed the classic pattern of decreasing catches and increasing effort as it approached and passed the tragedy point in exploitation of the stocks. Landings from Area 2, as the initial area of large catches off Washington and British Columbia came to be designated for management purposes (Figure 6), dropped from 30,000 tons in 1912 to 14,000 in 1923. In 1915, when landings reached what was to prove to be their high point through the next 30 years, fishers used 374,700 units of longline fishing gear, the measure of fishing effort used in this fishery. By 1923, gear used had increased to 488,500 units, indicating an expenditure of about 25 percent more effort than in 1915 in order to catch less than half the volume of fish. The price of halibut had gone up as landings decreased. Each fisher could now meet total costs with fewer fish per annum; more fishing effort could be supported despite an overall decrease in landings.

Management with Annual Quotas

The depletion of the Pacific halibut stocks did not continue to the point of virtual destruction of the fishery as it did with the Atlantic stocks. The drop in landings was too rapid and too short in the memory of fishers and government officials alike to be ignored. Canada and the United States signed a treaty in 1923 that established a resource management plan aimed at the restoration of halibut stocks. The first direct measures instituted under the treaty were a closed season from November 16 to February 15 and a program of scientific studies of the halibut stocks. The closed season had little effect as a resource management measure and understandably so. Fishing effort was already far too high for a three month closed season to have much effect on overfishing, especially when it came during the stormy winter months. The scientific study did produce knowledge that led to an effective resource management measure. By 1930, enough was known about the halibut stocks to permit prediction with confidence of the maximum amount that could be taken each year and still leave sufficient spawning stock to sustain yields at acceptable levels in subsequent years.

The two nations signed a new convention in 1930, and from 1932, an annual quota became the main management measure. The fishing grounds were divided into four areas for management purposes and annual quotas were assigned to each area. Once fishers reached the quota for a particular area, fishing had to cease in it for the remainder of the year. The new regime appeared to be accepted with little complaint. This was not surprising given the obviously overexploited state of the stocks, and the trust of fishers that the rules would be applied equally to all.

The quota system, in conjunction with lesser measures such as a minimum size for fish landed, proved effective in restoring halibut stocks. Landings increased from a near all time low of 21,700 tons in 1932 to an all time high of 35,200 tons in 1954. The fishing grounds had expanded since the previous high of 1915, so all of the difference in landings between 1932 and 1954 cannot be attributed to restoration of stocks that were depleted in early years of the fishery. No question exists, however, that the management program enjoyed considerable success. With no regulation, a repeat performance of the Atlantic halibut fiasco would have been the result.

The Halibut and Third Nation Fishers

The Pacific halibut management program gained world renown as the one example of successful management of a major ocean fishery resource. Its success was considered even more remarkable because it was an international fishery requiring the cooperative efforts of two nations. The United States and Canada were looked upon with some awe by the rest of the world for having done so well with Pacific halibut while equally sincere attempts elsewhere had failed.

A fundamental precondition for the success enjoyed through the 1950s is easily explained. The United States and Canada had, in effect, owned the halibut because fishers of no other nation could fish them profitably even though the stocks spent most of their lives in the international commons. Distance proved the main reason for this at first. Into the 1930s, the halibut grounds were too far from any other country to interest fishers other than those based on the west coast of Canada and the United States. Japanese fishers had created some consternation when they appeared in waters off Alaska late in the 1930s, but their operations were interrupted from the beginning of World War II until the peace treaty with Japan in 1952.

Just prior to the peace treaty, Japan, the United States, and Canada signed a fisheries treaty that called for Japanese abstention from fishing any stocks of the northeast Pacific Ocean that were fully exploited by the United States and Canada. Aimed primarily at salmon, stocks of halibut and herring also received specific mention in the treaty. The Japanese did later prove that some halibut stocks in the Bering Sea were not fully exploited and received the right to participate in harvest of them. The fishers of no other nation showed any particular interest in the northeast Pacific until the late 1950s.

The United States and Canada, by virtue of distance and the 1952 treaty of abstention with Japan, thus held *de facto* ownership of three fully exploited kinds of fish—the salmon, halibut with the aforementioned minor exception, and herring—in waters covered by the treaty. This included waters well beyond those under territorial control of the two nations. The halibut management program succeeded because the United States and Canada knew that benefits from investments in the

35

program would accrue to Americans and Canadians. Few, if any, similar *de facto* ownership situations had existed for any other seriously depleted fishery stocks of consequence in the history of marine fishing.

Conditions quickly changed with the boom in world fisheries exploitation beginning in the mid-1950s. Both Japan and the Soviet Union expanded their bottom trawl fishing fleets with vessels designed to fish profitably anywhere in the world. Prior to the mid-1950s, the rich bottom fish resources of the northeast Pacific were virtually unexploited except for Pacific halibut. Japanese and Russian trawlers began to exploit these stocks in international waters off the Aleutian Islands in the late 1950s and then moved on eastward and southward off the coasts of Alaska, British Columbia, Washington, and Oregon. Soon these trawlers were taking well over a million tons annually of species such as yellowfin sole and Alaska pollack. The Soviet Union, through an executive agreement with the United States, had agreed to abide by terms of the abstention treaty signed by Japan, Canada, and the United States, so neither Japanese nor Russian fishers targeted on halibut. They could not avoid, however, catching some halibut.

In 1959, the International Halibut Commission reported incidental catches of 894 metric tons of halibut by foreign (Soviet and Japanese) trawlers while fishing for other species of bottom fish. In 1960, the incidental catch of halibut jumped to 2,166 metric tons. All presumably were returned to the ocean in keeping with the treaty, but survival rates were low. Many were immature fish which meant that the eventual impact on the volume of halibut landings greatly exceeded the impact implied by tonnage figures alone. The incidental catch continued to climb but never reached as much as one percent of the total catch of the foreign vessels. To ask that these large catches of other fish in international waters cease in order to preserve the comparatively small halibut catches of United States and Canadian fishers was unrealistic; the treaty could not be stretched that far.

The incidental catches of halibut by Soviet and Japanese trawlers may have been small relative to the catches of other bottom fish, but they were large in terms of the annual halibut quota. United States and Canadian halibut landings began to decline. By 1976, the year before United States and Canada put their 200 mile fishery conservation zones into effect, their total halibut fishery landings had dropped to 13,500 tons, a far cry from the 30,000 ton landings recorded late in the 1950s and early in the 1960s. The International Halibut Commission had continued to regulate and impose quotas during the period of high incidental catches. Had it not done so, the Pacific halibut probably would have gone the way of those of the Atlantic. But the effect of the incidental catches must have weakened the incentives for management severely. Whether the United States and Canada would have continued the cost of doing so much longer is questionable.

Few halibut range farther than 200 miles from the coast so the new fishery conservation zones established by the United States and Canada restored their control over Pacific halibut beginning in 1977. Fishers who targeted on other species within 200 miles of the coast could now be forced to avoid large concentrations of halibut. Incidental catches of halibut by trawl fisheries have been greatly reduced; landings by the traditional halibut fishers rose as the stocks recovered. The quota was set at 34,400 tons in 1987. This is 2.5 times higher than landings in 1976 and equal to the levels reached late in the 1950s.

The United States and Canada are again demonstrating that cooperation between nations pays off in fisheries management if the investing nations can fully control access to the fishing grounds. Thanks to the 1982 Law of the Sea Treaty, the right to such control exists for all nations. The well-proven halibut model is being followed elsewhere based on national full ownership rather than the *de facto* ownership based on distance that made possible the initial success of the United States and Canada.

The Economist and the Halibut Quota System

The recovery of the Pacific halibut stocks between 1932 and the 1950s, and again since 1977, leaves no question that the biological effects of annual quotas can be positive. Rather than continued decline as with the Atlantic halibut, stocks in overfished areas were producing half again more on the average by 1950 than when quotas were instituted in 1932. The economic effects, however, dismayed economists who, as a professional group, have a high level of concern for the efficient use of capital, labor, and natural resources. The basis for this dismay was spelled out clearly in a now classic study supported by the Bureau of Commercial Fisheries (now the National Marine Fisheries Service) and published in 1962.[3] The study, prepared by professors James Crutchfield of the University of Washington and Arnold Zellner of the University of Wisconsin, found gross economic inefficiencies across the board. Far more capital in the form of vessels and gear and far more labor than needed were being expended to harvest the fish; the natural resource itself was being delivered to the consumer in much poorer condition than it could have been, and in smaller quantities.

The inefficient use of capital and labor was clearly indicated by the short time required to harvest the annual quota. In 1933, fishers needed 206 days to land the 11,000 ton quota of Area 2, and 268 days to land the 12,000 tons permitted to be taken from Area 3. By 1950, a 13,000 ton quota in Area 2 required only 32 days and the 14,000 tons from Area 3 only 66 days. The price of halibut had gone up as demand outgrew production. Proportionately more halibut fishers could be and were supported by the resource although far fewer could have harvested the quota, and could have done so more effectively.

A case can be made for having a closed halibut season during winter when the fish grow leaner, but no reason connected with the halibut or the market for them exists for not catching them during the rest of the year. By 1950, fishers had invested at least eight or nine times more capital in vessels and gear than was needed to harvest halibut in Area A and possibly four times as much needed for Area B. This resulted in the quota being taken soon after the fishing year began. Although the vessels could be used in other fisheries after the halibut quota was taken, they were designed for halibut and were less efficient in other fisheries than vessels designed for these fisheries. Nor did other fisheries exist in which all of the halibut vessels could be fully utilized when not fishing for halibut.

The economic waste associated with such an oversized fishing fleet understandably concerned Crutchfield and Zellner. They were equally appalled by irrational practices in the handling and marketing of halibut. A fish that could have been delivered fresh throughout the year ended up frozen in order to make it available during the long period remaining between the time that the annual quota was caught and the next year's quota became available. The shortness of the fishing period forced the fishers to fish with frenzy as they attempted to get a larger share of the quotas. The quantity of fish landed took precedence over quality. Halibut are tastier if bled, gutted, and iced immediately upon removal from the water. However, boats were coming in with unbutchered halibut lying on the open deck because fish holds were full, and fishers were pressured to capture as many as possible before the quota was filled and fishing had to cease. Some fish deteriorated to the point of being unfit to eat. The imperatives of the commons forced delivery of a lower quality product because it profited fishers to stress quantity even though doing so decreased the total value of the harvest to fishers and consumer alike. The total volume of landings also was somewhat lower since the quota was caught early in the year. If harvested throughout the year, that portion of the quota "stored" in the ocean would have added weight and have been marketed fresh. Instead, the fish gradually lost quality in freezer storage as happens over time with the freshest of fish no matter how carefully they are handled and frozen.

The problems associated with excess effort in the halibut fishery have increased since Crutchfield and Zellner's study. Seasons of a month or more in length such as existed in the 1950s have become a thing of the past. The fleet has become so large that managers find it difficult to stop the fishing when the quota is reached. For example, in 1983 a Southeast Alaska (Area 2C) quota of 1,700 tons was exceeded when fishers landed 3,100 tons in five days. The season closure was not fully effective until all the boats fishing when the whistle sounded returned to port and unloaded their fish. Presumably, so many boats were out that when all filled up and landed their catches, the quota had been exceeded by almost 100 percent.

In 1984, the quota for Area 2C was caught in three days; in 1985, in four days, and in 1986 in 3.5 days even though the quota had been increased to 5,300 tons or three times that of 1983 (Figure 6). The stocks were recovering rapidly from the effect of trawl fishing; excess longline fishing effort grew just as fast. Bruce Buls, writing in the August 1984 issue of *National Fisherman*, expressed the irrationality of it all as follows:

After the most recent run for halibut, it is again clear that the situation is a mess. The problem isn't that the fish aren't there, as is the case in some fisheries. In fact the resource appears to be in terrific shape. The harvest quotas have been climbing every year. Meanwhile, however, time on the grounds, price, and quality have fallen.

He continued by saying that effort had increased and with it:

. . . has come increased efficiency, thanks to the circle hook. And as more people have caught more fish, the International Pacific Halibut Commission has had to reduce the fishing time to prevent overharvesting. Last year, the first opening in the Gulf of Alaska was seven days. This year it was four. What will it be next year, 24 hours?

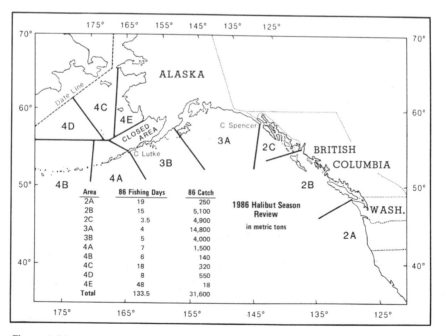

Area	86 Fishing Days	86 Catch
2A	19	250
2B	15	5,100
2C	3.5	4,900
3A	4	14,800
3B	5	4,000
4A	7	1,500
4B	6	140
4C	18	320
4D	8	550
4E	48	18
Total	133.5	31,600

1986 Halibut Season Review

in metric tons

Figure 6. Management areas for Pacific halibut with data on the fishery in 1986. (From *International Pacific Halibut Commission Annual Report, 1986*.)

In reference to effects of the imperative that fishers fish as hard as possible to get their share of the quota with quality suffering as a result, Buls wrote:

> I was in Kodiak the day after the season closed and saw fish being dressed at sea. Quality also suffers when you try to stuff 20 million pounds of halibut into the freezer virtually all at once. It doesn't fit. Consequently, the fish sits in the hold or on the fish-house floor until it can be frozen.[4]

Can one dispute Buls' conclusion, "the halibut is a noble creature that deserves to make it to market more frequently in fresh condition?" The International Halibut Commission has done well by fishers and consumers in keeping Pacific halibut flowing to market. Its management system based on an annual quota has been far better than no management. But can anyone imagine such harvest and marketing procedures for beef, pork, or poultry? Is there no answer from the economist as effective as the annual quota of the biologist?

The Halibut Fishery and Limited Entry

Crutchfield and Zellner accepted excessive fishing effort as the most fundamental problem to be solved in the halibut fishery. Reduce effort to the level needed for harvest and the consumer would receive a higher quality product and more of it. More important would be the improved efficiency in use of capital and labor resources. Waste avoided here could be invested in other economic activities to the ultimate benefit of consumers of products of these activities. Society at large would be well served in all respects.

As we saw in the previous chapter, the root of the basic problem, excess fishing effort, develops when a natural resource exploited in a common framework no longer meets human needs for its products. Two concepts that economists have given us, opportunity cost and economic rent, appear often in the economic literature on fisheries and add further understanding of the mechanics creating this excess effort and its tragic results.

Opportunity Cost and Economic Rent

Opportunity cost is the most favorable price that can be commanded by a factor of production. For example, let us imagine an independent trucker who operates his own rig valued at $100,000. Working fulltime driving and managing this rig, the trucker earns $25,000 annually. Let us also assume that if the trucker sold his rig, invested in a halibut longline vessel and gear of equal value, and worked fulltime as a fisher, income would rise to $35,000, or $10,000 a year more. The opportunity cost of the trucker's labor and capital is thus $35,000; $10,000 of it is foregone by remaining in trucking rather than using his or her capital and labor in halibut fishing. An opportunity for increasing income by this magnitude would attract many of us into fishing, especially if fishing appealed to us as an occupation.

Economic rent can be thought of as pure profit from a natural resource, that is, value gained over and above what one could reasonably expect to earn from labor and capital used to exploit the resource. For example, between 1973 and 1975, Alaska divided its salmon fishing grounds into 19 areas and instituted separate limited entry programs for each. Fishers who qualified for rights to fish an area received a license to fish in it. No additional licenses have been issued since. The license, or more precisely, the right to fish represented by it, became the personal property of its holder. The state charged a nominal fee for the licenses to cover the cost of issuing them.

Salmon catches in Alaskan waters increased after 1973 because of a combination of factors that include better management of the stocks and reduction of foreign fishing. Prices received for salmon have also increased rather markedly since 1973. Therefore, a larger number of salmon of higher value are now divided among the same number of fishers as qualified for a license in each area in 1973. In 1983, the average price of licenses ranged from a low of $4,948 for a hand troll license to $195,000 for a Peninsula/Aleutian seine license.[5] License holders were free to sell their license at the market rate. The sum received represented economic rent or pure profit created by controlled entry of salmon fishers for the area concerned. Had entry not been controlled, additional fishers would have been attracted into the fishery by opportunity costs commensurate with the economic rent.

Alaskan salmon fishery resources still are subjected to far more fishing effort than is needed. If the fleet is reduced to the approximate size required to harvest the annual quotas, one can imagine that the value of licenses would exceed the wildest anticipation of the license owners. Had someone owned the Atlantic halibut stocks, the volume of economic rent they would now be "collecting" because of increases in value of their fishery stocks through no effort of their own, that is, through growth in the market for halibut, also would be huge. The difference between what is and what could have been demonstrates the ability of the imperatives of the commons to cause overfishing.

The two concepts together help to explain why a natural resource exploited in a commons framework cannot produce pure profit, or at least not for long, and why resources in a commons framework come to be overexploited. As we saw in our model of a common pasture near London, as the city grew and income for farmers for dairy products went up, the opportunity for gain attracted more farmers to use the pasture. Continued increases in value of dairy products after the natural carrying capacity was exceeded, the tragedy point of common property, resulted in still more cows and consequent degradation of the pasture. Placement of the pasture in private ownership, on the other hand, would have enabled the owner to "collect" the economic rent associated with the increasing value created by a growing market. As we found, this would have worked to the advantage of consumers after the tragedy point was reached although common ownership may have given consumers milk at a lower cost before that point was reached.

Applied to the halibut fishery, we see that increasing value of halibut as markets expanded created a considerable potential for the creation of economic rent in both the Atlantic and Pacific fisheries. In both cases, opportunity costs associated with growth in demand for halibut attracted people from other occupations until the Atlantic halibut stocks came to be grossly overfished. Effort in the Pacific fishery, however, was matched to the productivity of the resource by annual quotas which resulted in extremely short fishing seasons. The increasing shortness of seasons noted earlier reflects the rise in value of halibut and a consequent increase in the amount of fishing effort. Increases in the market value of the fish increased the potential economic rent and in turn, the opportunity costs of persons such as the independent trucker described above. The result was far too much fishing effort.

The process is unavoidable as long as a potential for economic rent exists and anyone who can acquire the basic equipment needed is free to fish. If no restrictions exist that limit the number of fishing units, opportunity costs represented by the profits being made in the fishery attracts others into fishing. This continues until all of the potential rent is used to support the excess of fishers, and the greater the potential for rent, the greater the excess supported.

The process in all its irrationality from the standpoint of getting the most out of fishery resources is reflected in the 29th Annual Report of the Pacific Marine Fisheries Commission. The report states that the halibut catch in 1976 was 27.3 million pounds, or 300,000 pounds *less* than in 1975. Prices paid to fishers in 1976 averaged about $1.25 per pound. Total value of the catch was $34 million. This set a new record in value, far exceeding the 1975 value of $24 million and the previous record of $25 million set in 1972. To quote directly from the report, "The higher prices attracted many additional vessels into the halibut fleet."[6]

Need more be said? The total landings of halibut were slightly lower but consumer demand forced prices up to make the total value of these landings worth about 40 percent more than in the previous year. The fishery already had far more fishers than needed as shown by the short time required to catch the annual quota. The extra potential for economic rent created by the higher value in turn raised opportunity costs for people who did not fish for halibut in 1976, and encouraged them to become halibut fishers in 1977. As a consequence, the consumer most likely received even poorer quality halibut and possibly less of it. Do we need a better example to show why our normal concepts of how supply and demand affect production do not apply in a commons once the tragedy point is reached?

Development of Limited Entry as a Concept

Various measures other than quotas and closed seasons have been used to reduce fishing effort. The state of Maryland, for example, restricted Chesapeake Bay oyster harvesters to the use of sailing craft for many years after motorized vessels had become commonplace in other fisheries. Other examples include the prohibition of salmon purse seine vessels over 58 feet in length in Alaska, of electronic fish finders in Washington, and of spotter aircraft to aid in location of swordfish in California. Measures such as these impose inefficiencies and increase the costs of catching fish. Each fishing unit thus absorbs more of the potential economic rent that the fishery could generate, and reduces the number of fishing units that can be supported in the fishery.

Crutchfield and Zellner recognized all of these for what they were, imposed inefficiencies that create unnecessary waste of capital and labor in the harvest of fish. The heart of the problem, as they saw it, rested in excessive investment in boats, equipment, and labor; the most obvious answer was to reduce this investment. Match the fishing power of the fleet to the productivity of the resource and have them fish year round, or at least until biological or weather factors suggested otherwise. This would reduce shore-based processing and storage as well as fishing costs, and result in a better product.

The method advocated by Crutchfield and Zellner to do this was to license only as many vessels as were needed to harvest the resource in question. Deciding who was to leave the fishery would be a problem, but not an unsurmountable one. Another problem in a fishery as valuable as the one for Pacific halibut was that the division of the economic rent generated among the remaining boat owners would create large windfall profits for them. These profits would be considered inequitable by the remainder of society, but this would be a one-time event since the value of the licenses would be capitalized as licenses were bought and sold. First recipients of the licenses might become rich but the high value created would remove the potential for rent. With all the potential rent consumed by the value of the licenses, pressure on people in other occupations to become fishers and capture some of the potential rent would disappear. Economic resources formerly wasted in excess investment in vessels and gear, when those were the major costs of becoming a fisher, would then become available for more productive investment elsewhere in the economy. Rights to harvest represented by limitations on the number of vessels would become property rights, and property rights, as is demonstrated by other natural resources such as farm land, were essential to remove the tragedy of the commons.

Crutchfield was at the University of Washington, an institution of world renown for the study of marine fisheries. The overfished salmon and halibut resources of the northeast Pacific provided excellent proof of the need to take action. No authority on fisheries management questioned the theoretical soundness of the idea of limiting entry. It appeared to be an idea whose time had come; it soon had a substantial following under the leadership of Professor Crutchfield.

Limited entry as a concept was not new with Crutchfield and Zellner. It had been advocated as a conservation measure for some Canadian and United States fisheries before World War II, and a mild form was instituted in several Japanese fisheries from 1947 for reasons other than conservation. The crisis stage had not been reached in enough fisheries, however, to overcome various institutional barriers to its implementation before the war. Also, there was the ever present danger that successful conservation efforts by a coastal nation would increase foreign fishing effort just beyond territorial waters, that is, beyond control of the coastal nation. In the Japanese case, the economic stability of fishery enterprises, not resource conservation, was the dominant goal. This required only a slight reduction in the number of fishing units to give each enterprise enough economic rent to achieve the desired goal. Effort by Japanese fishers was not reduced enough to attract foreign fishers to the already heavily fished waters around Japan.

Distance, the treaty with Japan, and agreements with the Soviet Union did, as we have seen, combine to give to the United States and Canada *de facto* ownership of halibut, salmon, and herring in waters off their Pacific coast until the late 1950s. This *de facto* ownership sufficed to remove the worry about foreign fishers reaping the benefits of reduced effort through limited entry for two of these fish, salmon and herring. The third, halibut, were already severely decimated by incidental catches by foreign trawl vessels targeted on other bottom dwelling fish, and beyond the control of the international agreements. The fishing power of salmon fleets in both countries was far greater than needed, and that of the herring fleet was becoming excessive. These two fisheries met all of the basic criteria for limited entry, including the means to exclude foreign fishers from access to most of the stocks of salmon and halibut concerned. Overfishing of herring resources of the northeast Pacific began late in the 1960s. Canada imposed a limited entry system on its Pacific salmon fisheries in 1969, Alaska did the same in 1973, and Canada did so on its Pacific herring fishery in 1972. These three cases provide the longest experience with limited entry systems instituted for conservation purposes. A number of additional stocks have been brought under limited entry in the United States and Canada since these zones were established. Other countries, notably Australia and New Zealand, have followed suit.

Limited Entry Evaluated

Experience with use of limited entry, as can be seen from a brief history of its use, is still fairly shallow. Interest in the concept, however, runs high, and evaluation of its application in various forms to different fisheries has been continuous. The literature on limited entry now would fill a library shelf whereas in 1960 no more than the equivalent of a single

44

small volume was available on the subject. As a consequence, we can say that experience with it and scrutiny of this experience is adequate to form valid conclusions as to its effectiveness as a resource management measure.

The evidence leaves no question that limited entry as conceived by Crutchfield and Zellner has proved seriously wanting. Until very recently, all systems introduced for resources management purposes used the measures originally suggested, that is, measures designed to reduce the size and effectiveness of fishing fleets to levels approximating that needed to harvest the sustainable yield. The theory sounded good; implementation of it has proved impractical. In no case has a limited entry system reduced the fishing effectiveness of a fleet sufficiently to improve management of the resource. In most cases, the capacity of the fleet to harvest fish has increased.

The main shortcomings of programs to match harvest capacity with need began to appear soon after their implementation. Restriction on one aspect of capacity resulted in exaggeration of another. The British Columbia salmon fishery limited entry program used a reduction in the number of vessels to reduce harvest capacity. A reduction of 20 percent was attained, but the remaining fishers enlarged their vessels and improved their gear. A study published in 1984 states that, ". . . while the number of licensed vessels has declined by more than 20 percent, the capacity of the fleet has grown substantially along with capital investment. This has happened through the replacement of old vessels with newer, larger, and more technically efficient vessels and by the addition of new technology embodied in the gear deployed."[7] The Japanese tuna fishery program limited both the size and number of vessels. Vessels were constantly rebuilt to increase fishing effectiveness within the limits set. Crew quarters became more cramped to increase hold space. Fish holds were lined with plastic and used as fuel tanks on the way to fishing grounds in order to increase range. Fuel was stored on the decks in drums for the same reason. Smaller tuna vessels became less seaworthy with the stress on design within regulations to increase fishing capacity.[8]

Not unexpectedly, successful programs begot their own failure. An increase in profit to the remaining fishers gave them added incentive to increase the effectiveness of their fishing units and the money with which to respond to these incentives. They responded as would have most of us; they worked to further their own interests.

In retrospect, the lack of success of these programs is not surprising. Reducing harvest capacity of the fleet does nothing to remove the imperatives of the commons. The imperative to exploit the resource before someone else does is strengthened for those remaining by the greater return on efforts to do so. The imperative to take the best first is also strengthened. The imperative to forego investment that would improve productivity of the resource is unchanged except perhaps for small, localized fisheries where the fishers all know each other. The imperative to increase one's share by improving vessel and gear is also strengthened by the increased value of the fish one expects to catch.

Advocates of limited entry went back to the drawing board. An innovation resulted that removed the imperative to exploit the resource before someone else does. The innovation, known as individual fishers' quotas or IFQs, divides the total quota for the year among fishers holding harvester rights. The fishers now "own" a certain quantity of fish which they can harvest when and however they wish. This avoids mad rushes such as described above in the halibut fishery. It also encourages landing of a high quality product as the fishers strive to maximize income from the quantity of fish they now own. Proponents say that IFQs can help to reduce waste while fishing, that is, reduce the adverse effects of the imperative to take the best first, if the IFQs can be sold. Thus fishers who had a quota for widow rockfish but also ended up with halibut or salmon in their net would purchase quotas for these incidental or by-catches from someone else in order to be able to land them legally. Presumably the needed by-catch quota could be purchased, but the incentive to do so would be weakened by the price of the purchased quota. Most, if not all, of the economic rent from the salmon or halibut would go to the original quota owner. This means that the by-catches might be worth even less to the widow rockfish fishers than their own widow rockfish. If this were true, the economically rational course for the widow rockfish fishers would be to throw the by-catches away if widow rockfish were readily available to fill their boats.

With high value fish such as the salmon and halibut where larger fish are worth more than small ones, the waste is almost certain to be larger with than without IFQs. The IFQ holder would maximize the value of his quota by retaining only the larger and more valuable fish. This would be an advantage if the smaller fish released survived, but mortality rates on fish caught by commercial fishing methods are high. Waste is almost certain to occur unless uncharacteristic care is taken in handling and releasing the smaller, less valuable fish.

Readers can let their imaginations loose on the different types of limited entry in an effort to see how the imperatives of the commons can be weakened. My feeling is that the same conclusion will be reached that I reached once I started applying the imperatives to actual and hypothetical situations. I will, however, impose at this point a brief summary of one more study that became available to me in the summer of 1987.[9] If we had a similar study for every major fishery, I am sure the pressure for a change to full ownership would increase greatly.

Limited Entry and the Pacific Groundfish Fishery

The published account of the study is entitled *Limited Access Alternatives for the Pacific Groundfish Fishery*. The title describes the purpose of the study—to determine the best form of limited entry for this fishery.

A team made up of fishery management specialists from the Pacific coast research laboratories of the National Marine Fisheries Service, the Pacific Fisheries Management Council, and Oregon State University began the study in November 1984; the final version of the study was published in May 1987. The research on which conclusions were based was thorough; the analysis was excellent. The final recommendation was that IFQs be used to limit entry to the fishery. If one agrees that some form of harvester rights is the only answer, then the recommendation is fully acceptable. Data presented in the study, and conclusions drawn from them, however, leave no question that we would be better off with full ownership than with IFQs.

The fishers exploit stocks of about two dozen species of groundfish, including widow rockfish, in that part of the Pacific Ocean pastures of the United States between the Canadian and Mexican borders. The fleet in 1985 was made up of 357 otter trawl, 32 pot/trap, and 129 longline vessels. This fleet landed a total of 171,000 metric tons in 1985 valued at $69.9 million—about one-fourth of the value of all commercial landings from the ocean pastures off Washington, Oregon, and California. Room for an expansion of the harvest remains for some species whereas others are being overfished. The study was done in response to a request made in 1982 from trawl fishers for "an immediate emergency moratorium on all groundfish trawling." Since fishers understandably are among the last ones to call for such action, we can assume that a consensus existed that something needed to be done.

The team estimated potential economic rent under different conditions and costs to taxpayers. Expenditures by the federal and state governments for all aspects of management came to $10,156,300. The maximum economic rent obtainable was computed to be $12.6 million assuming a fishing fleet constructed, operated, and deployed " . . . as though there is a profit-seeking centralized manager of the fishery . . .," *in short, a full owner*. Under usual forms of limited entry, the potential economic rent is estimated to be about $8 million. No estimate was made of potential rent under IFQs since experience with this measure is so shallow. Presumably it would be higher than $8 million but less than $12 million.

If we accept ownership of the ocean pastures by the citizens of the country, no question exists of the advantages of electing to establish a full owner agency. Taxpayers spent $10 million to support the fishery and its resources in 1985; estimated economic rent under full ownership could have reached $12 million. Thus taxpayers and citizens have lost $22 million—$10 million in expenditures from the general fund and $12 million in economic rent foregone. With this much money to play with, we should be able to create a better deal for everyone. The full owner agency that we set up to manage the resources could be charged to maximize benefits but to leave no one worse off than at present. The agency would employ existing fishing enterprises to harvest the fish.

47

The fishing enterprises employed would be paid on the basis of harvest costs, not landed value. The imperatives of the commons would be completely removed. Some fishers might be employed to catch weed fish to alleviate problems of an unbalanced ecosystem resulting from selective fishing. Fishers would earn, on average, the same as they do now. Any fisher not able to earn as much from fishing as before the change could be compensated from the $12 million profit for a reasonable period of time. For fishers of retirement age, this could mean an income for the rest of their life. No one would be worse off than at present, most would be better off. Adverse disruption to existing fishing enterprises would be minimal.

The full owner agency probably would find returns on investment in improvement of productivity of the resources high enough to justify a substantial increase over that allocated out of the $10 million spent on management in 1985. The amount actually spent on research to understand and to improve the resource was $4.5 million; the remainder went for administration. Administrative costs could be reduced substantially through elimination of duplication between different levels of government now involved, and a reduced need to determine, allocate, and enforce an elaborate quota system. Shift of these savings to resource improvement should pay off in increased productivity.

It was pointed out to me in response to my plea for consideration of full ownership that IFQs could be auctioned off at full value to fishers.[10] This would capture all of the economic rent for the citizens at large. I replied that this would be closer to full ownership than to limited entry as the term is now used since fishers receive none of the economic rent. Fishers' incomes would, however, depend on the value of their landings. The imperative to take the best first thus would remain and wasteful fishing could result unless fishers were policed closely. Overseeing the auction of IFQs and policing fishing operations to prevent cheating would also mean higher administrative costs. A far more harmonious and effective relationship between owner and harvester will result if the high plains grain production model were to be followed.

The High Plains Grain Production Model

Any renewable natural resource under full ownership can be used as a parallel to fisheries to show the irrationalities of harvester rights. I use grain farming on the high plains of North America with students in my marine resources classes. It also makes a good summary of this chapter to bring home how full ownership can solve the problem used as the chapter title—Why Too Much Effort and How to Limit It—much better than can harvester rights.

Farmers of the high plains produce grain with an efficiency of labor and effectiveness of land use that would astound those who opened these lands to farming a century ago. Most of this grain is harvested by grain combining enterprises with an efficiency that would astound the original farmers even more. The resulting combination of farming and harvesting enterprises provides an apt example for fisheries. Full ownership rights in the marine habitat comparable to that of grain farmers of the high plains will provide the same incentives to effective management of the marine habitat that farmers have for their grain lands. The equipment used by fishers is as complex and expensive, or more so, than that used by grain combine entrepreneurs. The harvest equipment used in both cases is more efficiently used and probably better maintained than if the farmers or holders of full property rights to the marine habitat owned it themselves. The relationship between the enterprises that produce and those that harvest grain is a smooth one; no one talks seriously of changing it.

In our discussion of rights to harvest, I ask the students what would be the effect of granting rights to grain combining enterprises to harvest grain comparable to limited entry rights that have been granted to fish harvesting enterprises. Once they overcome their surprise at such a seemingly nonsensical question, their understanding is almost immediate. Grain production would drop in quantity and quality; everyone would be worse off except the first recipients of the grain combining rights. Second and subsequent holders of these rights would be saddled with debts that left them more or less in the same income position as combine enterprises before the rights to harvest were created. The first recipients would take their windfall capital gains and invest them elsewhere. As a consequence, both skilled combine entrepreneurs and capital would be lost to the grain business, lost not because their entrepreneurial skills or capital would serve anyone better elsewhere, but only because the first recipients no longer had sufficient incentives to stay in the business that they know best, grain harvesting. The students concluded, with sound logic I believe, that limited entry rights would have the same effect in fisheries. The first recipient of rights would be better off, but we were unable to think of anyone else that would. Most would be worse off.

Full property rights in the pastures of the ocean will lead to far more efficient and effective management of our fishery resources. The imperatives of the commons that result in too much fishing effort will be removed. The by-catch problems would be reduced because cost, not value, of harvest becomes the basis for remunerating fishers. Investment in harvest will be limited to effort needed just as in the harvest of grain, timber, cattle or any other products of a renewable resource managed under full ownership. No other system can be nearly as effective.

1   Quoted in Francis J. Captiva, "359 Years of Fishing," *Fishing Gazette*, 96 (November 1979):55.

2   George Brown Goode, *The Fisheries and Fishery Industries of the United States, Section V, Part 1, History and Methods of the Fisheries,* Washington, D.C.: Government Printing Office, 1887:3.

3   James A. Crutchfield and Arnold Zellner, "Economic Aspects of the Pacific Halibut Fishery," *Fishery Industrial Research* 1 (April 1962), 1–173.

4   Bruce Buls, "Halibut Season Goes Awry," *National Fisherman*, 65 (August 1964):7.

5   Alaska Commercial Fisheries Entry Commission, *The 1983 Report of the Commercial Fisheries Entry Commission*, Juneau: 1984.

6   Richard J. Myhre, "Review of the Pacific Halibut Fishery," *29th Annual Report of the Pacific Marine Fisheries Commission for the Year 1976* (May 1977):50.

7   R. Bruce Rettig, "License Limitation in the United States and Canada: An Assessment," *North American Journal of Fisheries Management*, 4 (Summer 1984):237.

8   E. A Keen, "Limited Entry: The Case of the Japanese Tuna Fishery," in Adam A. Sokoloski, ed., *Ocean Fishery Management: Discussion and Research*, Washington, D.C.: National Marine Fisheries Service, 1973:154.

9   Daniel D. Huppert, ed., *Limited Access Alternatives for the Pacific Groundfish Fishery*, Washington, D.C.:National Marine Fisheries Service, NOAA Technical Report NMFS 52, May 1987, 1–45.

10   Personal communication, Daniel D. Huppert, 1987.

4

New Tenure for an Old Resource

Biotic resources can become severely depleted under common property tenure, even—as we saw with the great auk and Steller's sea cow—to the point of extinction. The depletion came later with marine fishery resources than with major terrestrial biotic resources, but the tragedy of the commons clearly has arrived for stocks of the more valuable species of fish. No recent studies are available as to the degree that world fishery resources as a whole have been depleted, but that the level of depletion is serious and growing is not open to serious dispute. In the United States, which has one of the more effective fishery resource management programs, fisheries based on stocks harvested primarily in federally controlled waters must be brought under a Fisheries Management Plan if the stocks are fully exploited. At the beginning of 1987, 26 separate fisheries, two of which were added in 1986, were under management plans. Increasingly, these are stocks of species—such as squid—that few Americans considered to be food fish before the more desirable species began to increase rapidly in price in the late 1960s.

No one questions the irrationality of continued overfishing of valuable stocks of fish. A consensus also exists that by working with nature, we can produce more of the type of fish that we want just as farmers or foresters or ranchers get more of what they want from their land than would be produced by nature alone. Working with nature means just that, work. People do consider fishing or hunting or gathering wild nuts and berries to be fun. People even pay farmers to let them harvest fruit as a family outing. But working with nature to produce these things for harvest is seldom considered fun. To do so requires capital, which requires work to produce, and physical labor, a term that in no way connotes the fun of fishing or hunting or picking berries in summer.

Tom Sawyer may have enticed friends and acquaintances into working to whitewash Aunt Polly's fence under the guise of its being fun, but the long term commitment to working with nature to produce more of what we want requires a better and more lasting reward than Tom was able to offer.

Societies have solved the problem of getting individuals to work with land by assuring them the right to harvest, and to treat as their own, the fruits that their work helps nature to produce. This arrangement has worked well for agricultural, forest, and pasture lands, all of which were at one time open to use in common by all. The problem with fisheries is how to move from commons property tenure to arrangements that will make it worthwhile for people to work with nature to make the ocean pastures produce more of what we want.

We have spent considerable time and effort trying to find the appropriate arrangements for the oceans since the common property problem emerged full force in the 1960s. The creation of the EEZs was a major step in the right direction, but the rights systems being implemented within the EEZs to date are not. These are the limited entry systems, the rights to harvest, that do nothing to encourage people to work to help nature produce more fish. The warped investments made in attempts to compensate for the controlled aspect of fishing effort under limited entry show clearly that the imperatives of the commons described above (chapter 2) are not removed.

The rights needed for the ocean pastures parallel those that societies have developed for field, forest, and pasture in one major way. This parallel is ownership that permits full control of the production, harvest, and use, including sale, of commodities from the resource. This right does not necessarily imply that the same arrangements must exist across the board for fishery resources as for other resources. Both the optimum nature of the full owner agency, and the size of the ownership unit often varies with the resource. Forest resources, for example, with large capital and land requirements relative to labor needs, generally perform better if owned in large tracts by corporations or public agencies. Conversely, labor is relatively more important in agriculture; owner-operators usually apply their labor more effectively than do hired laborers. Family owned farms of a size that can be fully utilized with the labor resources of family members usually result in a more effective mix of land, labor, and capital than do huge agricultural estates such as are found in some Latin American countries, or in the collectives of the centrally planned economies. Given the need to establish rights for full control in fisheries, and realizing that the rights system does need to be fitted to the fishery resources, let us turn to aspects of the resource complex that bear keeping in mind while designing the optimum tenure system.

Rights and the Nature of Fishery Resources

Design of an optimum ownership system for fisheries requires more attention to the natural system than is necessary for agricultural, forestry, and grazing resources. Productivity of the latter three is enhanced by deliberate and often substantial modification of the natural ecosystem; in agriculture, the visible biotic portion of the ecosystem is changed completely. Most animal resource species associated with agricultural and grazing resources are domesticated and well adapted to appropriate degrees of confinement.

Fishery resource species, on the other hand, remain highly dependent on the natural ecosystem since all are, as yet at least, wild animals. The ocean pastures are beyond our ability to separate by fences as we do land units where fences provide for both confinement and exclusion of animals.[1] Many fishery resource species migrate over long distances to avoid seasonal temperature changes as well as to seek food. The marine ecosystem is complex and dynamic, and, compared to terrestrial ecosystems, it is as yet poorly understood by humans. Given these complexities and our present level of understanding them, let us turn to identifiable aspects that are important in the design of an optimal ownership system for marine fishery resources that are overexploited. Focus is primarily on the optimum size of the ownership unit. The marine fishery resource production and use complex is divided into its natural and human components to facilitate discussion.

The Natural Component

History shows that research to improve productivity of terrestrial resources can pay off handsomely. Productivity of agricultural resources increased steadily if slowly from the beginning of agriculture through empirical research by observant farmers on the lookout for better farming methods and crop species. Scientific research leaning heavily on laboratory methods, however, increased the productivity of agricultural resources more in this century than occurred in the millennium ending with the 19th century. Experience with scientific research in agriculture has been applied with considerable success in recent decades to improving productivity of forest and range resources. At present we are not able to manipulate the ocean pastures, or the species using them, to anything like the extent that we do with terrestrial ecosystems. However, our methodological base for research to improve productivity of renewable natural resources is large. Major developments that show promise in respect to fishery resource productivity are reported with increasing frequency despite relatively low expenditures in support of research in the field. The potential is large for creation of economic rent in fisheries by removal of the imperatives of the commons. A full owner of marine resources would find research to improve resource productivity a fertile field for investment for this economic rent.

No additional research is needed concerning constraints that the natural system places on the optimum size of the ownership unit for marine fishery resources. Our understanding is more than adequate to support design of this element of the optimum management system. The most important point to bear in mind is that management of any resource species is much easier if its entire habitat is under the control of one owner. If this criterion of our optimum system is to be fully met, the answer to the size of the optimum management unit immediately becomes clear; it must encompass all of the world's oceans. This is because the habitats of the different resource species overlap to such a degree that to draw boundaries around the habitat of one is certain to divide the habitat of others. This overlapping of habitats also means that ownership on a species basis seldom is desirable because the species compete for forage, which often includes each other, from the same pasture. Species by species ownership is certain to cause cattle rancher and sheepherder type conflicts for common property grazing resources made famous by Hollywood in movies depicting the Old West of the United States.

The rationale for a unified world ocean habitat can be demonstrated quickly by beginning with two stocks of fish, the albacore stocks of the North Pacific and the northern anchovy stocks of the east central Pacific. The northern anchovy range the waters of the California Current between Vancouver Island and the central part of Baja California. This population of anchovy appears to consist of two or three intermingling stocks. If the maximum benefits are to be obtained from the harvest of anchovy, these stocks and their habitats need to be under one owner. If the owner had a right to these fish but to no others in this habitat, management to maximize production of them presumably would include destruction of fish that feed on the anchovy. Among these are the North Pacific albacore, a fish that ranges across the mid-latitude portions of the Pacific between Asia and North America (Figure 7).

The market value of the albacore is over ten times that of the anchovy. Even if we assume that the albacore feed entirely on anchovy, and if 10 pounds of anchovy are needed to make one pound of albacore, a larger economic return will result if albacore production is emphasized over that for anchovy. The albacore in question, however, only eat the anchovy in question when they are in the California Current system, and even then eat species other than anchovy. Thus northern anchovy contribute only a small part to the weight of any individual albacore. If the anchovy and albacore were owned by different people, however, it would still be in the interest of the anchovy owner to destroy the albacore since they do consume anchovy in large numbers. In reference to net human benefits from the pasture, the albacore is the preferred species. We must conclude that maximum benefits will be gained from the two species if both are managed together.

54

Figure 7. Trolling for albacore tuna off California. "Longfins" are also a prime target for sportsfishers. (Photograph courtesy Ken Raymond, Southwest Fisheries Center, National Marine Fisheries Service.)

North Pacific stocks of these two species contribute only a small portion by either volume or value to world fisheries production. But they interact in inseparable ways with many others. To further tie these into other stocks of the same and different species, and to further complicate our overly simplified example in the process, let us continue with tuna species that have overlapping habitats. The habitat for bluefin tuna of the North Pacific overlaps the habitat for North Pacific albacore stocks. Bluefin migrate from one side of the Pacific to the other during their life cycle as do the albacore. On the western Pacific leg of their migration, they compete with albacore for food in the Kuroshio, or Black Current, off eastern Asia, and on the eastern Pacific leg for food in the California Current off North America. If someone owned the anchovy and albacore, removal of the competing bluefin would be desirable. But the bluefin is a far more valuable fish on the world market than is the albacore. Both bluefin and albacore are at the top of the food web and presumably of comparable gross ecological efficiency. Therefore, to manage the bluefin along with the albacore and anchovy makes good sense.

Let us continue. Southward on both sides of the Pacific, important stocks of yellowfin, bigeye, and skipjack tuna migrate northward with the sun to share the equatorward portion of the habitat of the cool water albacore and bluefin tuna, and to compete with these northern fish for anchovy and other forage species. Conversely, on their southward migrations, the tropical tuna intermingle with the albacore and bluefin stocks of the cooler southern Pacific waters. These albacore and bluefin stocks in turn mix with tuna and other marine resources of the Indian Ocean. The southern bluefin appear to belong to a population whose habitat includes the waters of the South Atlantic as well as the Indian and Pacific oceans. While in the South Atlantic, they mix with other cool water tunas of the South Atlantic, and as one goes northward, the pattern of mixing of tuna species found in the Pacific is repeated. Consideration of only a few species thus shows that division of the ocean pastures, or of stocks using these pastures, among owners is almost certain to affect adversely the management of a number of valuable stocks of fish. If the food chain and habitat linkages of all species are considered, then management of fishery resources obviously is complicated by any division of the oceans for purposes of ownership. If the linkages between fishery resources and their habitats alone are considered, management would be simplified if control of world fishery resources were placed under a single agency.

Land, unlike the oceans, is easily divided and fenced for various purposes including separation and ownership. The habitats of terrestrial wildlife resources, therefore, are divided and placed under separate owners with little or no reference to the wildlife. This enables the owners to use the land for purposes more remunerative to them, and presumably more valuable to society, than production of wildlife would be. Wild pheasants may feed on the remnants of grain crops left in the fields, but the main use of the land is to grow grain for the market, not pheasants. Conflicts often arise as anyone who has a garden next to a forest populated with deer well knows, but rarely is land set aside exclusively for the use of wildlife. Urbanization changes habitats so completely that few, if any, of the original wild species remain. In short, terrestrial wildlife resources usually lose out to more remunerative competing uses for their habitats.

Waste disposal and seabed mining are the only major uses of the oceans by humans, other than exploitation of marine biotic resources, that lead to serious modifications of marine habitats. Mining impacts usually end with extraction of the minerals or soon thereafter. Biotic resources are renewable; production of them can be sustained indefinitely. Extraction of minerals frm the seabed is a short-term activity by comparison with production of fish and other living resources of the ocean.

The conflict between the use of the oceans for waste disposal and fishery resources can be resolved to advantage. Much of the waste is organic material which, if properly placed, can enrich the pastures for ocean fishery resources and increase their productivity. Studies of disposal of Los Angeles area sewage in Santa Monica Bay, for example, show that sewage supports an estimated increase of the benthic biomass of the Bay of eight percent. Nutrients released from the sewage also are assumed to stimulate phytoplankton production, but the depth of release is so great that effects are unmeasurable by the time the nutrients released rise to the euphotic zone, the zone where sufficient sunlight penetrates to support plant growth.[2]

Human manure is, after all, much the same as the barnyard variety that we use so readily on our gardens, fields and pastures. Municipal sewage, if kept free of toxic materials and placed properly in the oceans, enhances production of fishery resources. The benefits from doing so should make it worthwhile for an ocean pasture owner to contribute to separation of land-generated wastes into those beneficial to the ocean ecosystem and those destructive to it. The beneficial "wastes" will then be placed in the ocean in a way designed to maximize benefits from them. Efforts will be made to dispose of the harmful ones in ways that assure no contamination of the ocean environment. Thus competition for the marine habitat is not, or at least need not be, a major problem as it is with wildlife on land. The main question then becomes whether ownership of the total ocean ecosystem under one agency is the preferred scheme in the total context of marine fishery resources production and use.

To summarize, marine fishery resources are almost all wild animal species, many of which range over wide areas. The habitat of any one resource species overlaps in part or in full the habitats of several others. Rights to the habitat of one wild stock or species cannot be assigned without creating a potential for conflict with owners of the habitats of other stocks or species. Similarly, assignment of separate ownership to individual wild stocks or species will create conflict over use of the habitat. Experience with wildlife on land provides ample proof that division of a species' habitat among different human owners complicates management of the resource. On land, we have chosen to make these divisions because doing so enables us to use the land far more profitably than if the land were managed primarily for wildlife.

The only long-term conflicting use of the oceans is disposal of wastes generated by humans. Division of the marine habitat helps little, if at all, in resolution of this conflict; however, a full owner of the marine habitat would work with the sewage disposal agency to resolve the conflict to the mutual advantage of each. As stated above, if one considers only the natural component of the marine fishery production and use complex, management of the entire ocean system as a single unit would be preferable. Attention to the human component, however, shows that subdivision of the oceans at national boundaries, with little reference to the effects this division will have on marine ecosystems, is essential to management of fishery resources of the ocean. Let us turn to the factors that make this compromise with constraints imposed by the natural component necessary.

The Human Component

The marine ecosystem clearly must be divided for full owner purposes when the human component of the marine fishery resource production and use system is considered. The need for division rests in two factors: (a) ownership requires support of a political system with effective and readily enforceable laws, and (b) coastal and offshore waters are of overwhelming importance to people who live adjacent to them and to the fishery resources of the oceans as well.

Meaningful full ownership can exist in modern societies only where it is supported by a responsive and enforceable system of laws. Relevant laws must be responsive to fishery resource management needs just as the laws of any city are to the need for management of automobile traffic or for protection of property. International law falls far short of meeting these needs. Management of the entire ocean ecosystem under full ownership would be possible only if an international agency were given sovereign authority over fishery resources along with the means to enforce this authority. No such arrangements are likely to be created. International law resembles gentlemen's agreements more than it resembles the law of sovereign nations, the concept with which most of us associate the word law. A full owner agreement for all the oceans' fish would involve too many "gentlemen;" such an agreement likely would be breached before the last signature could be affixed.

Turning to the second aspect, coastal and offshore waters play an important role in both the natural and human components of our ownership matrix. These are the fertile waters of the oceans. Fertility of the oceans depends primarily on upwelling of nutrient rich waters from below and into the euphotic zone—the upper layers of the ocean with enough sunlight for plants to carry out photosynthesis and get the food chain started. Locally, runoff from land also may increase nutrient levels significantly. Most upwelling and all runoff occurs along landward margins of the oceans. It is here that continental shelves, coastline configurations, winds, and the Coriolis Force combine and act upon ocean currents to bring about most of the vertical mixing that assures a flow of nutrients to the euphotic zone. The green waters of this part of the oceans produce ninety percent or more of the world's fishery resources because of this fertility. The blue waters of the high seas are deserts by comparison and of far less importance to our ownership considerations for this reason.

The importance of the human component/coastal water relationship, on the other hand, is simple enough but is seldom made explicit. Briefly put, it is the strong sense of possessiveness toward coastal waters that has developed in coastal populations over time. This sense is strongest for the intertidal zone and enclosed bays; it diminishes slowly with increasing distance from the coast. The rate of decrease depends on the strength of the relationship between the particular coastal population and the adjacent ocean. One would presume, for example, that the strength of feeling would be weaker and decline more rapidly for the aboriginal populations of southwest Africa, whose dependence on the oceans is slight, than for those of the Aleutian Islands, whose dependence on resources in coastal waters is almost total; or decline more rapidly for the people of Argentina, who have enough animal forage on land to produce meat more cheaply than fish, than for the Japanese, who have little in the way of terrestrial grazing resources.

In modernized, affluent countries, people have concentrated in coastal areas in increasing numbers, and have made the coastal zone their playground. On warm summer days, the numbers of waders, swimmers, surfers, scuba divers, sportsfishers, and boaters in or on the ocean near a major metropolitan area may approach the numbers of fish in these waters. This identification of coastal populations with the nearshore marine environment is too large a factor everywhere to be ignored. The relationship is too intimate. Imagine, if you can, the marine resources of the coastal waters off New England, in the North Sea, or along the coasts Japan under the control of an international agency with its headquarters in Rome or Nairobi. Even Grotius, the Dutch lawyer who argued so strongly for freedom of the seas, had to recognize sovereign control by coastal states over the marine environment along their coasts.

This zone, including territorial seas, enclosed bays, and saltwater marshes, must be effectively under control of full owners if fishery resources are to be managed effectively. It is an absolutely integral part of the nutrient rich coastal and offshore zone where most of our marine fishery resources are produced. Division of this all important zone for management under different owners can only complicate management of marine fishery resources. Division is difficult to justify except to gain the coverage of the effective system of laws that effective management requires.

The Compromise

Overlapping habitats of resource species mean that unified control of all of the world's living marine resources under one management is preferable only if the natural component of the resource complex is considered in isolation. Bringing in the human component rules this out. A compromise is essential.

An important step in the needed compromise has already been taken and accepted by the world community. This step was the extension of national control over fishery resources to a distance of at least 200 miles from land, and even farther under certain conditions. Most stocks of commercially important fish stay within 200 miles of land. The northern anchovy stocks discussed at the beginning of this chapter seldom get beyond 80 miles from the coast, but they go well beyond the three or twelve miles accepted by most nations as territorial waters. Twelve miles offers little help in the control of foreign fishing of these anchovies, but 100 miles probably would be ample, and 200 miles reserves the anchovy to the coastal nation with a good margin for safety. Highly migratory species such as the albacore and bluefin tunas make up less than 10 percent of world landings. Thus over 90 percent of marine fishery resources are now under established national legal systems.

Institutional arrangements to support the minimum-sized units, the national EEZs, called for by the compromise between our natural and human component are now in place. Minor adjustments outward do appear to be desirable in the seaward boundaries of a few EEZs where habitats of stocks that are primarily coastal protrude beyond the 200 mile limit. Notable examples are the cod stocks in the outer portion of the Canadian zone and hake stocks off Argentina. For the most part, however, further expansion of EEZs beyond 200 miles has little merit.

Three instances do remain where expansion and consolidation of management areas makes sense if the benefits associated with unified habitats are to be realized. These concern (a) stocks that migrate between the ocean pastures of two or more nations, (b) highly migratory stocks whose habitats include portions of EEZs but extend well beyond ocean-ward boundaries of them, and (c) resources under one nation's control for which jurisdiction is fragmented among national and lower levels of government. These are discussed separately below.

Transboundary Stocks

The need to divide the oceans in order to bring most marine resources under an effective legal system does mean that the rich coastal pastures must be divided at international boundaries. Needless to say, these boundaries were not drawn with ocean ecosystems in mind, and rare indeed is the boundary that does not divide the habitats of important stocks of fish. One nation is not likely to invest in management if fishers of the neighboring nation or nations sharing the stocks snap them up when they all cross the international boundary. Now that nations own all habitats within 200 miles of their coasts, they can jointly exercise control over stocks whose habitats are shared with adjacent nations. This gives nations sharing ownership an incentive to gain the benefits from management of larger ocean areas through cooperation with their neighbors.

The benefits of joint management of transboundary stocks are large enough to encourage most nations to work out cooperative agreements. The problems to be overcome in achieving these benefits do, however, vary widely. Where joint stocks are shared by two nations only and those nations have a history of friendship and cooperation, arrangements should come easily. On the other hand, where several nations are involved, which may or may not enjoy friendly relations, achieving the benefits of joint management will be more difficult.

The experience of the United States and Canada with shared stocks off their Pacific coasts illustrates the relative ease with which arrangements for transboundary stocks of two friendly nations can be established. As noted earlier, these two nations held de facto ownership of marine fishery resources in waters off their western coasts for many years. This *de facto* ownership, along with the close and friendly relations between the two nations, goes far to explain why salmon and halibut stocks of what is now their Pacific EEZs have been under successful joint management programs for many years.

Working out the complex treaty for sharing salmon stocks in rivers from northern California through British Columbia and into southeastern Alaska (Figure 8) understandably required involved and extended negotiations to complete. The problems associated with the natural history of dozens of separate stocks of five species of salmon presented a major challenge. Added to this is enmeshment of the international factor with historical friction among the four concerned states of the United States having partial jurisdiction over salmon that originate in rivers within their boundaries. That these complex natural and human factors were overcome suggests the magnitude of benefits to be gained through joint management. The benefits in this case, as can be expected in many others, were so large that eventual success was almost inevitable. The full meaning of the EEZ and of benefits that can result is yet to come for many nations. Once it does, one would suspect that arrangements for management of important transboundary stocks involving only two nations will be worked out even if the two nations have a history of relations marred by enmity.

Enclosed seas that are divided among the nations surrounding them contribute significantly to world fisheries production. To bring the fishery resources of these seas under one agency exercising full ownership would greatly simplify management of fishery resources in them. Two of these, the North Sea and the East China Sea, represent a wide range of potential difficulties to be overcome if benefits of unified management are to be obtained. Each of these seas has within it a number of valuable stocks whose habitats are shared by surrounding countries. Management of these resources through agreement among nations on a stock by stock basis as suggested for the two nation situations discussed above would be complicated indeed. For all nations concerned to relinquish control to a single agency assigned full responsibility for management of all stocks, including their harvest, would prove far more effective and efficient. Management would be fully unified; benefits would be divided according to the contribution of each country's waters.

The European Community moved toward unified management with formulation of its Common Fishing Policy in 1983 (Figure 9). This agreement falls far short of establishing full ownership under a single agency, but does move the Community in the right direction. Further developments toward single agency control of North Sea fishery resources are likely if relations between member nations continue to be harmonious in all major aspects. Relations are less than harmonious among nations

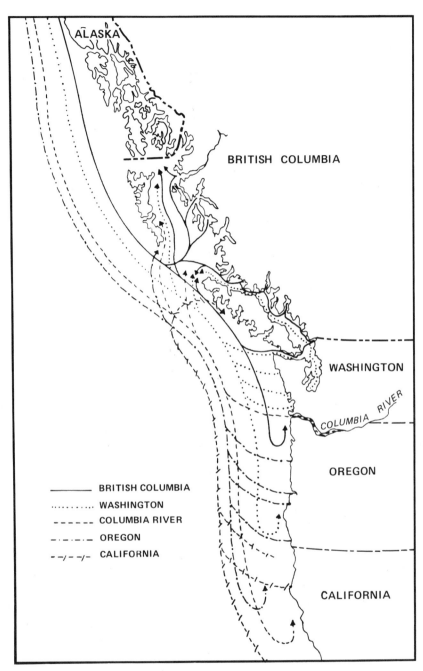

Figure 8. The migration patterns of chinook salmon from stocks of different rivers of western United States and Canada illustrate the complexity of managing transboundary stocks of salmon. (After Howard F. Horton, "Ocean Fishery Resources," pp. 55–78 in Susan Hanna, *et al.*, eds., *Exploring Conflicts in the Use of the Oceans Resources,* Oregon State University Sea Grant Program, 1980.)

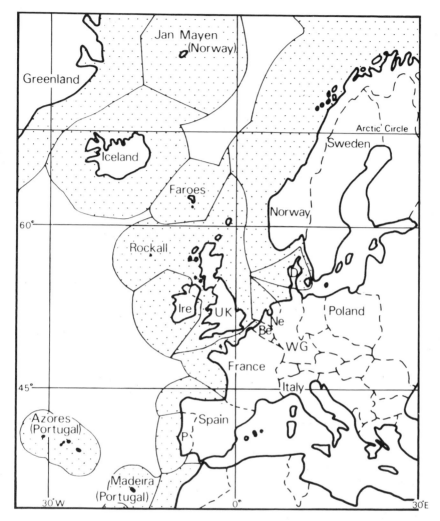

Figure 9. Exclusive economic zones of the northeastern Atlantic Ocean. Management of fishery resources is made difficult by fragmentation of the ocean such as is found here. (From Office of the Geographer, United States Department of State.)

sharing the East China Sea, and no prospect for an agreement similar to the Common Fishery Policy of the European Community appears likely in the foreseeable future.[3] Other factors being equal, however, the political complexities facing joint management under several nations are obviously far greater than for two nation situations.

Highly Migratory Stocks

Transboundary stocks as discussed above remain within the control of two or more nations. They are therefore under national systems of law at all times. The habitats of highly migratory stocks, on the other hand, extend into the high seas where the gentlemen's agreements known as international law provide the only legal support for fishery resources management. Portions of the habitats of highly migratory stocks that lie outside of an EEZ remain in an international commons. Therefore, incentives for the coastal nations to invest in management are lacking for highly migratory stocks because harvest of these resources is open to fishers of all nations while they are in this commons.

A possible solution to the international commons problem would be to vest ownership of that portion of the habitats of highly migratory stocks within the international commons in an international agency. This agency could then enter into agreements with nations that share the habitat of a specific highly migratory stock. For example, about 60 percent of landings from the yellowfin tuna stocks of the eastern tropical Pacific are caught in the EEZs of coastal nations from Mexico to Peru inclusive; 40 percent of the landings are from international waters (Figure 10). Experience with management of the yellowfin stocks under the Inter-American Tropical Tuna Commission shows that fishing outside of waters under control of a managing agency is extremely difficult to regulate. The expectation of this happening again if the coastal nations were to develop a management program deters them from even considering such a course of action. If an international agency held ownership of the international portion of the yellowfin habitat, it could enter into cooperative arrangements with the coastal nations to bring the entire habitat of the eastern tropical Pacific yellowfin under one agency. Arrangements for a management program based on full ownership of the entire stock could then be worked out.

Admittedly, working out effective full owner arrangements for even such relatively localized stocks as the yellowfin tuna of the eastern tropical Pacific will be complex. Among other things, changes will be needed in the Law of the Sea, ways must be devised to manage stocks on a species basis that overlap habitats of other stocks managed as part of the total resource complex in a individual EEZ, and much more research must be done on stocks that are not as yet very well understood. Suffice it to suggest here that the benefits are sufficiently large to justify efforts to do so.

Unified National Control of Fisheries

Some nations have divided jurisdiction over their ocean pastures between national and lower level governments. These arrangements date from the time when fish were plentiful, and the interests of governments were limited largely to keeping statistics on fishers, how many fish were caught, and what happened to the fish after landing. This made sense prior to the overfishing that developed when fishery resources began to run out. Fishing itself was primarily a localized activity. Administrative matters associated with it could be carried out effectively

64

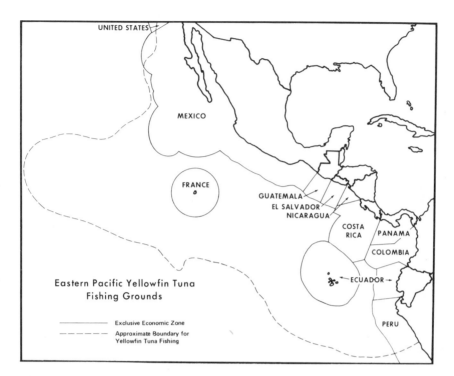

Figure 10. Yellowfin tuna fishing grounds in the eastern tropical Pacific Ocean would require an amendment to the Law of the Sea in order to establish a management agency based on full ownership. (From E. A Keen, "Common Property in Fisheries," *Marine Policy,* 7 [July 1983], 197–211.)

by lower level governments. Fishery resources were plentiful and therefore required no management. When overfishing began under the common property framework, the concern of governments changed abruptly. Fishery resources management became the focus of governments; keeping up with fishers and fishing became secondary to this larger concern.

Resources management calls for a much broader spatial perspective than does looking after fishers and their landings. As noted above, the optimum size of a management area is the largest area that can be brought under a responsive and enforceable system of laws. This means that at the minimum, the fishery resources of each physically separate area of all marine waters under a nation's control should be under unified control.[4] Where relevant, enlargement of these national minimum sized units can be made by combining adjoining national units. Effective unified management becomes, by reason of the need for the largest management area feasible, a responsibility of national level government. Delegation of this responsibility to lower levels of government is difficult to justify.

The United States provides excellent examples of the irrationalities created by fragmented control of its marine pastures. The Fishery Conservation and Management Act (FCMA) provides for basic division of control between federal and state governments at the territorial seas boundary. States have management responsibility for all fishery resources exploited primarily within territorial waters, that is, from the mean low tide line (coastal baseline) along open coasts to a distance of nine miles for the Texas and west Florida coasts and three miles for all others. All resources are under full state control when within internal marine waters, that is, for bodies of ocean waters with restricted connections to the ocean such as Chesapeake and San Francisco bays. Basic responsibility for management decisions about fishery resources that are exploited primarily within the EEZ[5] rests with fishery management councils set up under the FCMA (Figure 11). A Fishery Management Plan (FMP) for each resource requiring management is developed by the council responsible in cooperation with the states concerned. This must be approved by the Secretary of Commerce after which it is implemented primarily by state agencies in state controlled waters and by federal agencies within the EEZ.

The division between state and federally controlled waters is a critical one. The state controlled portion includes all of the estuarine and coastal water habitats of marine fishery resources of the country. On a per unit of area basis, this is by far the most important portion of the fishery resource habitat. Data compiled by the National Marine Fisheries Service's Fishery Ecology Program in 1983 showed that 68 percent by

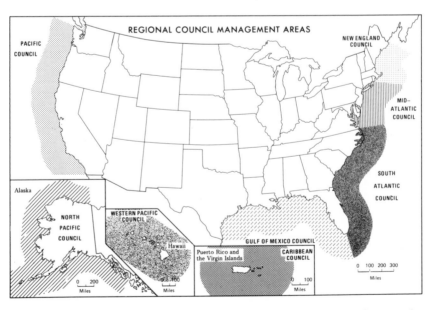

Figure 11. Fishery management council areas as established by the Fishery Conservation and Management Act. (Cartography by Barbara Aguado.)

volume and 58 percent by value of the nation's marine fish landings were accounted for by species fully or partially dependent on estuarine habitats. Stocks of some of these species are exploited primarily in the EEZ while others are exploited primarily within the territorial sea. Most, however, are exploited on both sides of the territorial sea boundary. The role of state controlled waters in the health of the nation's marine fishery resources is indeed an important one.

The states have not performed well in management of the resources under their control. Shortcomings in state management are widely recognized. The shortcomings were discussed by Professor James Crutchfield at a lecture given at Scripps Institution of Oceanography in 1986. In paraphrase, Crutchfield said that the states' role in fisheries management is demonstrably a disaster everywhere. Decisions on stocks that cross state boundaries dividing the territorial seas, and this includes most stocks on the Atlantic and Gulf coasts, are almost always too slow in coming if they are made at all. The least competent or least conservation oriented states call the terms. Professor Crutchfield has served for several years on the Pacific Fisheries Management Council in addition to being a long term student of fisheries management.

Division of territorial waters off the 48 contiguous states among 21 coastal states adds substantially to the fragmentation of marine habitats. Also, control of a few internal marine water bodies, Chesapeake Bay being the most important, is divided among states. Managing stocks that migrate across state boundaries in both internal and territorial waters is sorely hindered by these divisions. Three marine fishery commissions— one each for the Atlantic, the Gulf, and the Pacific coast states—that were formed in the 1940s to coordinate state management of shared stocks have helped but little. Two locally important resources, the striped bass of the Atlantic and the redfish of the Gulf, illustrate the difficulties in the interstate and state/federal management of marine fishery resources.

Atlantic Striped Bass

The striped bass has been described as a noble fish that is the aquatic equivalent of the American eagle. It is a favorite of sports and commercial fishers from North Carolina to Maine. Commercial landings reached an all time high of 7,350 tons in 1973, after which time they dropped steadily to 850 tons in 1983 (Figure 12). Accurate data on striped bass landings by recreational fishers are not collected, but, as one fisherman testified in 1984, fishers who once caught five in a day are now lucky to see five over the course of the summer. In 1984, Congresswoman Claudine Schneider of Rhode Island introduced legislation to impose a three-year federal moratorium on fishing for striped bass with a provision for its extension to five years if needed.

Public hearings on Representative Schneider's bill were held 20 March 1984. One only needs to skim the print of these hearings to realize how completely this noble fish had fallen through what was described

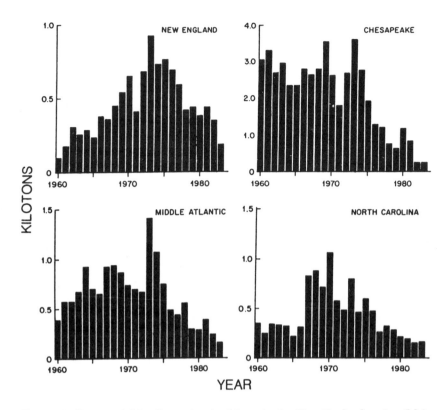

Figure 12. Commercial landings of striped bass in the New England region (Maine through Connecticut), the Middle Atlantic region (New York, New Jersey, and Delaware), the Chesapeake region (Maryland and Virginia), and North Carolina, 1960–83. Stocks have shown some recovery under a federally mandated management plan started in 1984. (Graphs from John Boreman, "Stripped Bass Research and Management—How Far Have We Come in 25 Years?," pp. 25–36 in *Recreational Fisheries and the Environment*, National Marine Fisheries Service, Sandy Hook Laboratory, 1986.)

as a gaping rend in the wildlife management scheme. The main issue in the hearings was not whether the moratorium was needed (everyone agreed that it was), but whether the federal government should assume control or continue to trust the states to work out a management program adequate for restoration of the stocks.

Stocks of the Atlantic striped bass that spawn in the Hudson River, rivers emptying into the upper Chesapeake Bay, and the Roanoke River provide most of the striped bass caught by Atlantic coast fishers. Three states—New York, Maryland and North Carolina—are thus responsible for this most critical part of the striped bass life cycle. The annual migration of the striped bass extends from their spawning grounds to the open Atlantic and then through waters off the coasts from North Carolina to Nova Scotia. They are harvested throughout the range of their annual migration. They are caught primarily in state controlled waters but are taken occasionally in the EEZ.

As a fish exploited primarily in state waters, management of the striped bass is a state responsibility. The 11 states responsible for the management of the Atlantic coast striped bass stocks asked the Atlantic States Marine Fisheries Commission to develop a management plan when landings began to decline in the 1970s. The plan required approval by all 11 states before it could become effective. At the time of the 1984 Congressional hearings, two states had not approved the plan so it was not yet in operation. The resources continued to decline despite the importance of striped bass to the citizens of the state concerned and appeals from these citizens for action.

The Atlantic Striped Bass Conservation Act that resulted from Congresswoman Schneider's bill required the Atlantic States Fisheries Commission to develop and coordinate implementation of a plan for the striped bass. The plan was to be worked out in cooperation with the Bureau of Sports Fisheries and Wildlife and the National Marine Fisheries Agency, the federal agencies most concerned with fisheries. The Act required approval of the plan by all states concerned by 30 June 1985 with certification of continued compliance by each state every six months thereafter for the life of the Act. The Act also called for an immediate and complete moratorium on all fishing if implementation of the plan was found to be inadequate. Federal funds were allocated to support the Plan and for state and federal agencies to carry out joint research programs to develop additional information needed to manage the resource.

Congressional hearings were held in February 1986 on whether to extend the Act. Testimony presented left no doubt that such progress as had been made depended strongly on the coercive conditions for compliance placed on the states by the Act. Two reasons why states were reluctant to comply stand out. One was pressure from interest groups on their state governments. The governor of New Jersey, for example, signed the Plan on the last day possible, presumably because fishers resisted the 24 inch minimum size imposed by the Plan. The other obvious reason was a lack of funding. An excerpt from the testimony of the Commission's Executive Director illustrates this problem. In reference to funds for the Commission's use in implementing the Plan, he stated:

> . . . when the money runs out, I will make efforts to have the States contribute more, but it has been a very slow job. I have been with this Commission for 15 years and I also have been associated with it since 1952, and it is very parsimoniously fed by its member States. We just don't have money to operate. People can believe that as they will or not. There are only two permanent employees in the Commission.[6]

The interests and feelings of responsibility of the states concerned were just too diverse to overcome the problems growing out of the fragmentation of the habitat of the striped bass. The impetus for action and funds to support it had to come from an agency, the national government, in which a sense of responsibility for the entire habitat was unified (Figure 13).

Redfish of the Gulf of Mexico

The redfish, or red drum, is an important recreational and commercial resource of the Gulf states. Commercial landings of redfish reached 2,400 metric tons in 1976, the largest volume recorded to that time. Louisiana landings dominated with 1,000 tons followed by Texas with 900 and Florida (west coast only) with 400 tons. Accurate data for recreational landings are not available, but they apparently exceed commercial landings by a substantial margin. An estimate for 1975, for example, credited the recreational fishery with landings of over 12,000 tons. Decreased catch rates after 1976 led Texas to restrict harvest of redfish from its waters to recreational fishers only from 1981. Alabama followed suit in 1984.

Much of the redfish spawning takes place in federal waters by schools of large redfish. The larvae drift into coastal and estuarine waters where they remain at least until they are through the juvenile stage. Unlike salmon and halibut, large redfish are less valuable than smaller

Figure 13. Spawning striped sea bass in an experimental hatchery program at Hubbs Marine Research Center, San Diego, California. California has a stronger incentive to invest in striped sea bass hatcheries than do the Atlantic Coast states since the habitat of the bass is entirely within waters off California. Striped bass were introduced into California waters from the Atlantic coast late in the 1800s. (Photograph courtesy Don Kent.)

ones. The fisheries, both commercial and recreational, thus targeted the more valuable young adult fish found primarily in state controlled waters. Large adult fish, most of which remain well offshore, are prolific spawners. Their existence gave assurance of continued restocking as long as they went largely unexploited. The Gulf redfish are presumed to be all of one stock, but the extent to which individuals migrate is not known. Thus the degree to which overfishing off one state would deplete the resource in the waters of other states remains in question.

Strong fears developed in 1986 that overfishing of the large fish in federal waters would provide a chance to determine the hard way the effects that fishing in federal waters would have on the fish population in state waters. A recipe for blackened redfish, Cajun style, developed by a chef in New Orleans quickly gained national fame and created an explosion in the demand for redfish. Commercial landings rose to almost 4,000 tons in the first half of 1986, more than 50 percent higher than the previous annual peak. A majority of these were taken from the schools of large fish in federal waters. The threat to what had been considered a reserve brood stock nearly created a pandemonium in Gulf fishing circles.

Like the striped bass, the redfish is a species caught primarily in state waters, and its management had been left to the states. The Gulf of Mexico Fishery Management Council and the Gulf States Marine Fisheries Commission published a joint study on the resource and its fishery in 1984.[7] The Council had not, however, prepared a Fisheries Management Plan for redfish nor did it show evidence of responding to the emergency by planning to do so. The states have no direct control over fishing in federal waters. They can, however, control fishing within waters under their control and landings within their boundaries regardless of the origin of the fish. Texas and Alabama had forbade sale of redfish within their boundaries before the 1986 crisis arose. Had Louisiana, Mississippi, and Florida chosen to do likewise, the states could have effectively controlled exploitation in federal waters by refusing to permit landing of commercially caught fish. They did not choose to do so either by direct cooperation or by working through the Gulf States Marine Fisheries Commission.

Moves toward controlling this potentially disastrous expansion of commercial exploitation of redfish again came from the House Committee on Merchant Marine and Fisheries. Louisiana Congressman John Breaux, chair of that committee's Subcommittee on Fisheries and Wildlife Conservation and the Environment, introduced a bill titled The Redfish Conservation and Management Act of 1986. Hearings on the bill were held 2 June 1986 in New Orleans with Representative Breaux and another Louisiana congressman, Billy Tauzin, the only Committee members present. The bill, which called for an emergency FMP for the redfish, galvanized the Secretary of Commerce into action. A 90 day emergency quota of one million pounds (a little under 500 metric tons) was imposed late in June. This quota was caught in less than one month. No commercial fishing for redfish in federal waters was permitted after that. The National Marine Fisheries Service and the Gulf of Mexico Fishery Management Council worked hard and delivered an emergency fishing plan on 23 December in time for Christmas. The FMP limited redfish landings from federal waters to a small quota for incidental catches by shrimp boats. Louisiana, Mississippi, and Florida continued to permit commercial fishing in their waters. Commercial landings for 1986 reportedly reached about 6,000 tons, by far the highest on record. An amendment to the redfish FMP became effective in October 1987 that, among other things, severely limits commercial fishing for redfish in the EEZ off Gulf Coast states.

Whether the Gulf states would have done better with redfish in the longer run than the Atlantic states did with striped bass may never be known—the emergency rescue by the Merchant Marine and Fisheries Committee is likely to be permanent. No question exists, however, that they did not respond with the timeliness that fishery resources management requires. Questions can also be raised as to what would have happened if a representative from outside the Gulf region had been chairing the Subcommittee instead of Congressman Breaux of Louisiana. Leaving emergency actions to a Congressional committee concerned with a wide variety of matters is a rather risky way to manage a fishery resource.

Stocks in Federal Waters

Overfished stocks exploited primarily in federal waters fared little better than those in state waters in the early years of the FCMA. Preparation and implementation of FMPs on such stocks are the joint responsibility of the councils and their member states. States are expected to realign their own regulations to fit those of the FMP and to help enforce the latter. Some states were reluctant to do so at first. In a FCMA oversight hearing held in 1982, for example, it was pointed out that Maine had no restriction on the amount of cod, haddock, or yellowtail flounder that could be caught in state waters. The FMP for these stocks set an annual quota that required fishing for them to stop once the quota was reached. Maine did not enforce the quota. Not unexpectedly, reports of catches of these species from Maine waters shot up and reports of catches from the EEZ ceased once the FMP quota was filled. Enforcement at sea is difficult. Most of the fish were caught in federal waters but were reported as having been caught within state waters. In addition to having the quota exceeded, getting erroneous data on place of catch must have made the fishery managers unhappy.

On the Pacific coast, salmon management has been made more complex than it needed to be because of wrangling between the Pacific Fisheries Management Council and the states of Washington, Oregon, and California over closed seasons in state waters. This finally resulted in use of the right of preemption of state control when Oregon persisted in permitting salmon fishing after closure dates set by the salmon FMP.

Management of stocks exploited primarily in federal waters improved as these early problems were ironed out. Squabbles between states over allocation of annual quotas, however, still impede both development and enforcement of FMPs. This is likely to continue as long as representation on the councils remains unchanged. Each state now has at least two voting members, the state's chief fisheries officer and one other appointed for a three year term from a list submitted by the governor of the state. These members serve at the pleasure of the governor. They respond to pressure from interest groups within their states as a consequence. Since the members representing states have an overwhelming majority vote, matters of conflict among interest groups in the different states often require a majority of the council's time to resolve. These matters often have little or nothing to do directly with management of the fishery resources. More often they concern such things as allocation of quotas and differences over open and closed seasons desired by different state user groups. Resolution of these conflicts also require an inordinate amount of staff scientist time as they try to fit various options to resolve these conflicts to the realities of the resource. Various measures to resolve these shortcomings have been recommended for the next round of revision of the FCMA. State government representatives, however, have had a strong voice in revisions to date. Unless their electorates call for new directions, the advantages of fully unified management are unlikely to be achieved.

States' Rights—Is the Price too High?

Citizens of coastal states unquestionably would receive more benefits from fishery resources off their coasts if management of these resources were unified. The only argument set forth consistently for a continued state role in the management of marine fishery resources is that states' rights should not be weakened as a matter of principle. Testimony of Representative Stan Schleuter of the Texas State Legislature at the June 1986 redfish hearings is typical. He insisted that the states can do the job, that "We, as state lawmakers and fishery managers from Texas, are not willing to allow the federal government to step in and usurp the state's authority to manage a fishery found predominantly in state waters."[8] The plea is based in ideology, not an assessment of the states' record in management nor of the impediments imposed by fragmenting jurisdiction over habitat in response to this ideological concern.

Do benefits from maintaining states' rights justify the loss of benefits from the better management that could result from giving up the states' role? Reasons for retaining state ownership of seabed mineral resources include major monetary return to the state treasuries from them. Oil resources within territorial waters off Louisiana, Texas, and California are owned outright by these states. Revenues from them make major direct contributions to the state coffers, state residents pay lower taxes as a result. Fishery resources management, on the other hand, results in a net outflow from the state general tax funds. In the study of the Pacific groundfish fishery cited in chapter 3, the estimated direct cost for management in 1986 was $542,800 for Washington, $854,000 for Oregon, and $981,300 for California for a total contribution from the states of $2,378,100. The only direct return to the state coffers from this fishery was a nominal sum from fishing license and landing fees. Citizens of these states could have more and better fish from the groundfish resources if the states turned management over entirely to a full owner management agency. They would also save themselves a drain on their tax monies by doing so.

Constitutional issues are not involved in the question of states' rights to marine resources off their coasts. These were settled in decisions of the Supreme Court of the United States in 1947 and 1950 concerning rights of California, Louisiana and Texas to petroleum in territorial waters adjacent to them. In the 1947 decision in the United States v. California case, the Supreme Court ruled ". . . that California is not the owner of the three-mile marginal belt along its coast, and that the Federal Government rather than the state has paramount rights in and power over that belt, an incident to which is full dominion over the resources of the soil under that water area, including oil."[9] The states sought to legalize their control through legislative action. The coastal states, including the Great Lakes states, had the majority in Congress needed to pass a bill giving ownership to the states. President Truman gave notice that he would veto any such bill. The Republican platform in the 1952 presidential elections promised that such a law would be signed. In 1953, Congress passed and President Eisenhower signed the Submerged Lands Act that gave ownership of both seabed and water column resources in territorial waters to the states.

No doubt exists that coastal states have the majority in Congress to do pretty much as they wish with marine resources if the President concurs. Since the Submerged Lands Act was passed, this majority has been increased in the Senate and House by the addition of two coastal states, Alaska and Hawaii, and in the House by migration of population to coastal states. States are unlikely, however, to take over full ownership of resources in the entire EEZ off their coasts. The ideological implications of this for national unity would be too adverse. A better ideologically based response would be for the citizens of coastal states to recognize marine fishery resources as national resources, assume a stewardship role for the privilege of easy access through proximity, and relinquish all claims to a management role to a unified management agency. In return they would gain the real economic benefits of no longer paying management costs from their state taxes and of having more fish available for food and recreation. Most citizens will opt to move in this direction if they take the time to understand the issues. I believe that they will find their time well spent if they do so. The caution against fragmenting fishery resource habitats any more than necessary is well worth heeding.

1   Pen culture, which has proved effective in the aquaculture of numerous species does, of course, in a sense involve fencing off part of the ocean. Pasturage, however, is not involved. The practice more closely parallels feed lot operations for cattle than it does pasturage where the animals harvest their own forage rather than having their feed brought to them.

2   Willard Bascom, "The Effects of Sludge Disposal in Santa Monica Bay," in Virginia K. Tipple and Dana R. Kester, eds., *Impact of Marine Pollution on Society*, South Hadley, Massachusetts: J. F. Bergin Publishers, 1982:233.

3   See Mark Wise, *The Common Fisheries Policy of the European Community*, London: Methuen, 1984, for a good treatment of the development of the European Community's marine fisheries management policies and structure.

4   For anadromous fishery resources, extension of control over fresh waters where the stocks spawn is also desirable.

5   As a matter of convenience, the EEZ of the United States often is referred to as if it included all marine waters of the country. Legally, it includes only the area between the territorial sea boundary and a line drawn 200 miles from the coastal baseline from which the territorial sea is measured. Advocates of expanding the United States' territorial sea boundary to 12 nautical miles, the line used by most countries, have grown since the Law of the Sea Treaty was completed in 1982. Whether the states will gain control over fisheries to a new boundary is one of the major issues that will have to be settled if a decision to expand the boundary is made.

6   U. S. Congress, House of Representatives, Committee on Merchant Marine and Fisheries, *Fish and Wildlife Miscellaneous—Part Four, Hearings before the Subcommittee on Fisheries and Wildlife and the Environment of the Committee on Merchant Marine and Fisheries*, 99th Congress, 2nd session, 7 February 1986:146.

7   Gulf of Mexico Fishery Management Council and Gulf States Marine Fisheries Commission, *Fishery Profile of Red Drum*, Tampa, Florida: Gulf of Mexico Fishery Management Council, 1984.

8   U. S. Congress, House of Representatives, Committee on Merchant Marine and Fisheries, *Redfish, Hearings before the Subcommittee on Fisheries and Wildlife Conservation and the Environment of the Committee on Merchant Marine and Fisheries*, 99th Congress, 2nd session, 2 June 1986:9.

9   Quoted in John M. Armstrong and Peter C. Ryner, *Ocean Management: A New Perspective*, Ann Arbor: Ann Arbor Science Publishers, 1981:25.

5

The Benefits of Optimum Tenure

The ultimate benefit that we can expect from unified management of marine fishery resources under a full owner agency will be more fish of the species that we prefer. This means better fishing for recreational and commercial fishers and less costly fish for consumers. Whether prices of fish to the consumer will become as close as they were to the price of chicken in the early 1960s is doubtful. Under the more effective management made possible by full ownership, however, bringing the average price of fish in line with the average price of beef and pork should be fairly easy to accomplish. Consumers will also find better quality fish available with removal of the incentives of the commons and the irrational fishing practices that these incentives engender. Taxpayers will fare better as fisheries become self supporting and funds start flowing from fisheries into the public coffers rather than in the opposite direction.

The purpose of this chapter is to suggest ways to ease the transition to full ownership and to sum up potential benefits of doing so. Long term benefits are difficult to assess at this stage, and some may think my discussion below concerning benefits is overly optimistic. The inadequacy of our knowledge of the ocean ecosystem does invite caution, but we are learning fast. The incentives for, and funds to support, additional research will increase under full ownership. Measured against what we have done with terrestrial ecosystems, my assumptions of what can be done by working with the ocean ecosystem seem conservative.

My optimism as to our ability to devise a workable full owner system is also subject to challenge. Full ownership will require profound changes in institutional arrangements. The changes in ownership were equally profound, however, for other resources as societies moved from the harvest-only incentives of the hunting and gathering stage to the production maximizing incentives of full ownership. The transition can be a painful one as the history of struggles over common pastures in Great Britain and in the American West shows. It need not be. Properly understood beforehand and planned with a firm understanding of what is needed, the transition can be made to the benefit of all and at no economic cost to anyone. Let us first look at the immediate benefits and how they can be used to ease the transition.

Immediate Benefits and Funding the Transition

The change in investment incentives to those of full ownership will create immediate and substantial benefits. Excess fishing effort, as noted earlier, is the major problem we face today in fishery resources management. We simply pay more than necessary to have our fish harvested and end up with fewer fish because of this excess effort. Economic rent, often potentially large, is dissipated in overfishing as higher prices induce expansion of fishing effort to levels beyond that needed to harvest the stocks. For example, a study made late in the 1960s estimated that the total catch from fishery resources of the North Atlantic Ocean could have been taken with one-third less effort. Professor Crutchfield, commenting on this study in 1980, suggested that the needless costs involved in the harvest of fertile North Atlantic waters could be in the neighborhood of *$4 or $5 billion.*[1] As noted earlier, estimates such as Professor Crutchfield's of potential economic rent wasted through excess fishing effort are all too rare, and more are needed. The one on North Atlantic fisheries has not been updated, but if it were, the amounts would be higher now than they were in 1980.

Professor Crutchfield also co-authored a study published in 1969 in which estimates are given of the value of effort wasted in harvesting Bristol Bay salmon.[2] World War II salmon catch rates, when overfishing was reduced by the war, were used in the study to estimate the minimum effort needed to harvest stocks that are not overfished. Based on their findings for the wartime period, the authors estimated that excess effort ranged from 33 percent in the 1934–36 period to 83 percent in the 1955–59 period. The remote location of Bristol Bay relative to other salmon fishing grounds suggests that excess effort rates for United States salmon fisheries as a whole must have averaged somewhat higher.

The ex-vessel price received by salmon fishers increased substantially during the 1970s. Inflation contributed to this increase, but a substantial part of it was an increase in real value as demand grew worldwide, and especially in Japan, for salmon. The growth in real value provided incentives to add even more unnecessary effort than was used in the 1950s. Thus to use the 83 percent rate for recent years should give us a conservative estimate of the cost of effort wasted in the salmon harvest.

Funding the Transition in the United States

NMFS data place the value of United States salmon landings in 1986 at $494 million. Accepting the axiom that a common property resource produces no rent, the entire $494 million, except for a small portion collected by fishers under Alaska's limited entry system, was consumed in the harvest of the salmon. Applying our conservative excess effort rate of 83 percent, and with a generous allowance for rent collected by Alaska's limited entry program, we must have spent at least $300 million more than needed on the 1985 salmon harvest. The federal government spent about $150 million on marine fisheries management in 1986; the states probably spent an equal or slightly larger amount. Thus the potential rent from salmon alone could have covered all governmental expenditures for management of all marine fisheries for 1986. The funds actually spent, of course, came from general tax funds, not directly from the fisheries.

No study comparable to that noted above for salmon has been done for halibut, another high value species of the northeast Pacific Ocean. However, the short season required to take the annual quota described earlier suggests that the level of excess effort expended in catching halibut equalled or exceeded that for salmon. The annual volume of halibut landings falls well short of that for salmon; the estimated value totalled only $83 million in 1986. Calculated conservatively at the 83 percent excess effort rate used above for salmon, this still gives a sum of $69 million foregone in economic rent—enough to cover almost half of the National Marine Fisheries Service budget for 1986. Perhaps a better use of it would have been to pay fishers to not have expended the excess fishing effort and to have avoided the irrational fishing practices that go with excess effort. Had this effort not been expended, consumers would have had better quality halibut and perhaps more of it. The retail price may have been a little higher because of the higher quality of the product, but differences in the cost of harvest would have had no effect on halibut prices to consumers.

The more valuable the species, the larger the effort wasted in harvesting it is likely to be. The majority of food fish stocks harvested by United States fishers could be caught with substantially less effort than is now expended. The proportion of effort wasted was, of course, lower on average for the whole than for the more valuable species like salmon, halibut, lobsters, shrimp, striped bass, and swordfish. However, we can assume that the proportion of effort wasted by United States fishers because of the imperatives of the commons at least matches the one-third waste of effort cited above for North Atlantic fisheries. NMFS statistics show the ex-vessel value of domestic commercial landings of edible fish and shellfish in 1986 to have been $2.64 billion. One-third of this is $880 million, a substantial amount of economic rent with which to begin funding the transition to our optimum management system.

The sum of $880 million represents money that could have been saved through a reduction in fishing effort alone. Improved direction of fishing effort could also create significant benefits soon after full ownership became a reality. Harking back to the halibut example, fish would be landed in reference to market demand, not in order to get a larger share of the quota. Quality, not quantity of fish landed on any one trip would be stressed, and fish would remain in the ocean to grow and be delivered fresh when needed rather than stored in freezers because the annual quota was caught in a few days. Turning again to salmon, the two most effective methods for salmon fishing—traps and wheels—are now almost completely forbidden because they are too efficient. Use of these to the extent possible would reduce the direct costs of fishing, assure that the fish would be harvested at their optimum size, improve handling during the harvest process, greatly shorten the period between removal from the water and processing, and markedly simplify control of escapement for breeding purposes. The result would be a larger volume of fish, better quality fish, and, of course, fish of higher unit and total value.

An increase of 10 percent in total value of United States fishery landings through improved direction of fishing effort and handling would seem reasonable, and at no increase in cost of harvest. This would have given an additional $264 million in economic rent for 1986. Added to the $880 million from savings in fishing effort, $1.1 billion in economic rent would have been created in 1986. These funds represent savings from the excess effort that would not have been expended and from more rational fishing and handling of fish in reference to market factors. The only loss worthy of note would have been the loss of income to fishers associated with elimination of excess fishing effort. This lost income would have been substantially less than the gain in economic rent.

Easing the Transition and Short-Term Benefits

No one should suffer a loss of income as a result of the change from common property to full owner tenure. The most important use that could be made of economic rent such as the $1.1 billion described above would be to use as much of it as needed as a fund to ease the transition. All fishers should be assured that their take-home income from fisheries would not be reduced from what it had averaged before the change. Fishers choosing to leave fishing should be paid on the agreed upon base income for a number of years—or for life, if necessary. Those choosing to remain as harvesters of fish should be assured that any shortfall of income below the agreed upon base would be made up from the transition fund. Compensation also should be paid to supporting industries such as boat builders if they show a loss of income caused by the change.

The change in method of compensation for harvesting fish would date from establishment of full ownership. Harvested fish would belong to the full owner agency, not to the fishers. The incentive of the commons that induces fishers to fish hard and fast to get the fish before someone else, and the incentive to take the best first, would be gone. Contracts probably would best be let, on an open bid basis, for a specified volume of a certain species or mix of species to be harvested within a fixed period. This period would be of sufficient length to permit fishers to work reasonable hours under safe weather conditions. Harvest contracts would carry stipulations to provide for landings of high quality fish harvested by methods in keeping with good resource management practices. Otherwise, fishers would be free to choose the method of fishing used. Warped investments in vessels and gear associated with limited entry systems would be avoided completely. Incidental or by-catches would be compensated for at the same rate as the target species, or at rates slightly higher or lower as needed to avoid waste of these species, or to discourage deliberate efforts to catch them. Thus the basis for compensation for harvesting fish would, in principle, closely parallel the basis for compensating grain harvesting enterprises described earlier in the grain belt model.

The number of fishers compensated from the transition fund would decrease with time until all harvesters remaining would be full free enterprise entrepreneurs in the same sense as the grain combine enterprises used as an example in chapter 3. Entry and exit from fishing would be uncontrolled as in any other legitimate occupation in a market controlled economic system. The animosities between fishers and resource managers associated with the allocation of rights would no longer interfere with good resources management. No one would be worse off for the change if it is carried out equitably. With passage of time, the stream of benefits would grow as improved management encouraged by the incentives of full ownership increased in its effect.

Mid-Term Benefits

The short-term benefits result from the elimination of irrational fishing practices while stocks are still in an overexploited condition. Benefits will continue to grow as stocks recover and are harvested with the more rational methods that accompany full ownership. As a rule of thumb, productivity of stocks of all commercial species will increase in proportion to the degree that they have been overfished. For stocks that have not been overfished as yet, the only increase in benefits will come from improved direction of fishing effort. A mid-term increase in landed value of 50 percent probably could be achieved within a decade. Unit value and prices to consumers should decline as the increased production brings down prices.

The Long-Term Potential

The short- and mid-term benefits discussed above would come from working with natural stocks as they are at present, that is, with little or no effort being made to modify the ecosystem or the resource species in order to increase productivity of desired species. Experience with terrestrial biotic resources suggests that a great potential exists for enhancement of output of the products we want through manipulation of the ecosystem and of the genetic structure of the resource species. This means moving beyond natural levels of productivity of the desired species by helping them to compete for food on the ocean pastures. It also presupposes that the ocean pastures themselves can be induced to produce more through measures such as increasing the quantity of nutrient salts in the euphotic zone. This would enable plants to fix more of the sun's energy and broaden the base for productivity at all levels of the food chain.

The following discussion of possibilities for enhancement through true husbandry must of necessity be based on informed guesswork given the lack of specific supporting studies. The investment opportunities associated with running out of fish from natural stocks are too recently upon us, the present institutional arrangements too adverse to capitalizing on these opportunities, for much thought to have been given to such possibilities. But experience with terrestrial ecosystems suggests that the following scenario can be realized easily if the incentives of full ownership are activated.

Enhancing the Competitiveness of Resource Species

The major work done by hunters and gatherers in order to obtain products they desire from biotic resources is to harvest the products. Eventually, these removals begin to affect the ability of the desired species to compete with less desirable species. Thus begins the sequence of overuse that too many cows imposed on the pasture in the common pasture example given in chapter 2. The imperatives of cows to take the best first cannot be changed, or at least no one has as yet trained cows to do so. We can do so with human hunters and gatherers, including fishers, by changing the harvest incentives to those of full ownership. We can then take the next logical step and enhance the food supply of our most desired species by removing competitors as we do on terrestrial pastures.

Gunderson drew an analogy between the American bison and the decline of fishery resources in his article, *The Great Widow Rockfish Hunt of 1980–1982*, implying that we are wantonly decimating the fish as we did the bison. But do we really want to bring the bison back in the numbers that existed before their decimation by humans? The cow has been shaped through selective breeding over the ages to be a far better instrument for converting pasture grasses into products that we want than is the bison. The cow, however, can no longer compete with the bison or other wild competitors without the help of humans.

At one time cows did compete with other wild species. As they became domesticated and genetically changed to benefit humans, they

82

required more and more aid from their owners in order to compete for a place in the pasture's animal community. The owner's, and society's, reward for providing the assistance was a larger return from the pastures. In time, we also found it to our advantage to not only remove competitors for forage but also to manipulate competition among forage species of plants to counter adverse effects of the take the best first imperative under which cows graze. The adverse effects of the take the best first imperative are countered by the owner investing in work to remove less desirable or inedible species. In short, we do work to manipulate ecosystems to produce more of what we want than if nature takes its own course.

Can we not anticipate parallel, or at least similar, developments for ocean pastures? A farmer or rancher who depends on improved pasture, as most do, may invest more effort in removing weed species than in the crop species. Would experimentation along these lines with ocean ecosystems be worthwhile?

Such experimentation scarcely seems worth hoping for unless we move under full owner incentives for managing the ocean pastures. To refer back to our grain harvest example, no farmer would consider the tremendous investment needed to enable domesticated grains to compete with weeds in the highly modified ecosystem that is his grain field if someone else held the rights of harvest. We even have trouble getting the federal Office of Management and Budget (OMB) to budget funds to manage national grazing lands properly. The reluctance of OMB lies partly in who gets the economic rent. Ranchers claim they have the right to use these lands, and manage to do so for fees below the market value of forage harvested by their animals. The difference between the fees they pay and the market value of the forage is the economic rent given to them. If ranchers paid market value, the return from fees might exceed the costs of management and convince the OMB that funds to improve the rangelands are a good investment. Improved management would result in increased productivity which would in turn increase the market value of the grazing privileges. The OMB rationally would respond to the profit motive and invest as long as the return on the investment was worthwhile. The pasture resources would become more productive, and the price of beef would become lower as production increased. From the standpoint of the OMB, fisheries research now represents a one way flow outward from the national treasury. OMB's perspective would be reversed under full ownership of the ocean pastures.

The ocean ecosystem is extremely complicated and poorly understood as yet. Care should be taken therefore in assuming that a major direct link exists between only two species in it. We do have instances, however, where removal of less desirable fish species probably would prove to be of immediate benefit. New England small boat cod fishers, for example, complain that they have difficulty taking their fair share of the cod quota because dogfish eat the cod off their hooks. We can also presume that dogfish compete with cod for forage. To reduce the dogfish population would thus have a doubly positive effect on production of cod. Fewer cod would be eaten by dogfish; fewer dogfish should mean more forage for cod. Dogfish were at one time harvested as a source of liver oil, but cheaper substitutes were found, and they have not been harvested since. A full owner, however, might find removal worthwhile for the same reason that a farmer finds removal of weeds, or a rancher of predators on his livestock, to be worthwhile. A full owner would also find research to increase knowledge of the workings of the ocean ecosystem to be a good investment.

The relevance of changed incentives that go with full ownership is too clear to be ignored. Reducing the population of dogfish will not take place under a commons framework with unlimited access or with harvester rights without a near total subsidy for the cost of doing so (dogfish, if landed in quantity, presumably would have some value for animal feed, fertilizer, or possibly low cost food products for humans although far less than needed to defray the total costs of harvest).

Under a system of harvester rights, the subsidy for removing dogfish and other weed species logically could come from fees on the fisheries enhanced by removal of the dogfish. However, collecting and allocating such fees would, as experience shows, require a great deal of energy on the part of fishery resource managers. The process also would leave feelings of animosity and antagonism that would impair needed cooperation between managers and fishers. Under a full owner, removal of dogfish would be worthwhile to fisher and to owner. Whether viewed as an unwanted weed or predator, their removal would be as much a matter of common sense on the part of the owning agency as it is for the farmer and rancher.

Improvement of Species Productivity

The productivity of the different species of domesticated plants and animals available to the modern farmer and rancher owes much to selective breeding by farmers and ranchers through the ages. However, scientific breeding carried out by specialists using techniques developed within the past century has proved to be a far faster way to breed for greater productivity of plants and animals. Little has been done with marine biotic resources in the way of genetic improvement of species. Surely geneticists can apply the accumulated knowledge of genetic principles to achieve results far more quickly than took place over the ages with animals and plants for agriculture.

The results of the little work that has been done with fish suggest that investment in research in species improvement can pay handsome returns in a short time. Work with salmonids, for example, suggests that with our present day knowledge of genetics, productivity increases equivalent to centuries of selective breeding by farmers and ranchers can be accomplished in a few years or at most, a few decades. The institutional framework for marine resources at present does little to encourage funding the research needed to take advantage of these opportunities. Under full ownership, research and development would be carried out as long as economic benefits resulting were large enough to justify doing so.

Efforts to date also suggest the potential that exists in the tremendous fecundity of fish. Under natural conditions, mating pairs of most fish species lay and fertilize millions of eggs, a vast majority of which are eaten or lost in other ways before they hatch or pass through the larval stage. Dependence on natural conditions for the reproduction of wild stocks means that we must maintain a large proportion of the adult stock for breeding purposes. Natural salmon runs, for example, require an escapement of about 50 percent of the adult salmon returning to their parent stream if that stock is to be maintained. Use of hatcheries reduces the required escapement for brood stock to about 15 percent. Thus a 35 percent increase in total harvest is achieved in return for helping salmon get through the egg and larval stages, the time when they are most vulnerable. Investment in hatcheries has proved to be a good investment in most cases. Benefit:cost ratios of around six to one were cited to me in Japan in 1979 for salmon hatcheries there. How many among us would be tempted to forego lunch in order to invest the money saved for a return of that magnitude?

At the turn of the century, American fishery scientists became infatuated with the idea of taking advantage of the natural fecundity of fish. Sizeable investments in hatcheries for a variety of species resulted but had little or no visible effect on harvestable resources. "Once burned, a wiser person" is a good adage, but we know more about the marine environment and how fish and their young fit into it now than we did then. Salmon hatcheries paid off poorly until the 1960s because of poor survival rates. Survival rates have been improved substantially since then. Development of hatcheries for species that spawn at sea will prove more difficult than for anadromous species like salmon that spawn in fresh water. Experiments with floating fish hatcheries in the open ocean where fry can be reared and released under optimum environmental conditions would be fairly costly. Under present arrangements, funding for such research comes with difficulty. The possibilities of success with seagoing hatcheries may be high enough to encourage experimentation, however, if the returns on the investment are assured to the investor. Our full owner agency would have that incentive and the financial wherewithal to act in response to it.

Integrated Resources Management

During the energy crisis of the 1970s, the federal government funded experiments in waters off San Diego to produce energy from giant kelp. The envisaged kelp farm was to be fertilized with nutrient-rich water artificially upwelled from below the euphotic zone. Kelp, from which energy, animal feed, and fertilizer may eventually be produced competitively, was the goal of the experiments. The project faded away with the decline of the energy crisis. That the upwelled water, being cooler than that in the euphotic zone, sank before the kelp plants could make use of it contributed to ending the experiment, but the fall in oil prices probably was the main reason.

Increased production of fish was expected to result from the San Diego kelp farm. Had the value of the fish been added to the benefits package, the project would have had a better chance even with the fall in oil prices. Unfortunately, the fish moved back and forth from waters under United States' control to what were international waters at the time and open to exploitation by anyone. Thus enthusiasm for including fish in the benefit:cost analysis for the kelp farm was weak. Had the fishery resources been under a full owner agency, such as the EEZs now make possible, that agency surely would have considered carefully participation in the kelp experiment.

Are present institutional arrangements for marine resources causing us to miss even better opportunities for integrating management of different resources than were those offered by the kelp experiment? Disposal of thermal wastes is a major problem faced in the generation of electric power with fossil fuel or nuclear energy. Without question, the oceans can handle these wastes more easily than can fresh water streams or lakes. However, once-through cooling systems for coastal power plants now take water from near the surface, heat it, and return it to surface waters at temperatures that may do considerable damage to marine life. Fish often collect in this warm plume of water only to be killed by the sudden chill that takes place when the plant is shut down for repairs or other reasons. Large volumes of water are moved through the cooling system; marine organisms, including eggs and larva of valuable fish species, move through with it. Few survive the trip.

Sites suitable for power plants exist along our coasts from which cooling waters from below the thermocline, that level at which temperatures decrease sharply, can be pumped. Water below the thermocline usually contains more nutrient salts than does water at the surface; fewer marine organisms are found in it than in the surface water. This cooler water could provide the cooling function needed in the power plant and then be discharged at the surface at lower temperatures than do present designs. This would reduce the two major adverse effects of power plants on the marine ecosystem—discharge of water at high temperatures and destruction of life passing through the cooling system. The nutrient rich water would remain on the surface, not sink as did the cold water of the kelp farm experiment described above. Forage for fish would be enhanced; the net effect of the power plant use of cooling water on marine life might be positive, not negative as at present.

A cooling system as described above might cost substantially more than those of conventional design. Benefit:cost analysis in the integrated framework of marine biotic resources and electric power production, however, could prove to be positive. A full owner of the marine pastures would actively seek out the power plant owner to determine whether joint investment in deeper intake lines would be mutually beneficial. It is difficult to imagine such action being taken under present institutional arrangements. Fishery resource managers of state and federal agencies, and of the fishery management councils, lack incentives to do so. Nor is a power company likely to take on the task of convincing public agencies responsible for fisheries to contribute to the scheme. The company would find it easier to convince its state utility commission to raise power rates to cover the higher net costs of conventional systems.

Ocean thermal energy conversion (OTEC) offers similar potentials. The possibilities of integrating power and fish production appear far more favorable in this context than with kelp. The low temperature differential exploited with OTEC requires the artificial upwelling of truly tremendous volumes of nutrient rich water. Temperature differences suitable for OTEC are found only in tropical waters, waters in which the high sun energy levels assure almost immediate use of nutrients by plant plankton in the euphotic zone. Experiments using upwelled water to produce shellfish in the Virgin Islands resulted in high levels of production in ponds on land. Use in place of fertile water upwelled by OTEC plants, as was attempted with the San Diego kelp farm experiment, is more practical than use of this fertile water in ponds on land. As with coastal power plant cooling systems, the water is warmed and remains on the surface. Fishery production down current from an OTEC plant will be enhanced substantially as energy from plants using these nutrients moves up the food chain. The value of the fish produced might approach that of the electric power. A full owner agency of the affected fishery resource would be quick to react to such an opportunity and help in construction of OTEC plants. Fish and power would be cheaper as a result. Nothing is likely to happen, however, as long as the fish are unowned until captured.

Sewage disposal provides a final and obvious area for integration of uses of the marine environment. The problem of disposal of sewage in fresh and salt water hounds all levels of government with increasing insistency for a solution. In reference to effects on marine ecosystems, the design of ocean disposal systems presently stresses avoidance of adverse impacts. Designs that include attention to the beneficial aspects of sewage might help defray costs of construction of the disposal system through higher production of fish.

Sewage is made up primarily of organic matter, that is, of manure and other compostable materials. Night soil, or human excrement, is a major source of fertilizer in many subsistence farming regions of the world. Comments by scientists and lay persons alike on such use are usually positive. Productivity of ocean waters, like that of the land, can be raised markedly with appropriate addition of these wastes. Recreational fishers and scientists who have studied the effects of sewage disposal in the ocean are well aware of this. Ask any party boat captain in southern California or researcher with the Southern California Coastal Water Research Project, an agency established to study sewage disposal in the region, where the most fish are to be found. The answer likely will be, "Over the sewage outfalls."

Here again, a single agency owner of the fishery resources would be quick to recognize the opportunity. Design and construction of sewage outfalls to enhance fisheries production, not just to reduce adverse impacts on the environment, might well be subsidized by the fishery resource owner. Similar help in the design and operation of sewage treatment systems to reduce inputs of materials harmful to fishery production could also be expected. These opportunities are not likely to be realized under a common property or limited entry framework for fishery resources.

Reduction of Subsidies

Incomes of fishers tend to be low and unstable in all societies. This instability stems from the wide variation over time in availability of fish, and from the ease with which one can become a fisher. When prices drop to low levels because of overproduction or because fish becomes scarce, the economies of fishing communities become depressed. Fishers find building up a nest egg in prosperous times to carry them over hard times to be difficult. This is because prosperity attracts additional people into the fishery until incomes on average fall to levels just adequate to cover costs. A consequence of this income instability, and of a romantic view of fishing as an occupation by other members of the society, is a higher level of subsidies to fishers than their political influence as measured by numbers alone would suggest.

Fishery enterprises should become more economically stable under a full owner system. Under the incentives of harvester rights, fishers tend to invest more heavily in the means of harvest than may be wise in order to compete for shares of the harvest. Under full ownership, the incentive for fishers to gamble on good catches of high value fish would be removed since the fish would not belong to the fishers. Returns on capital and labor to fishers would be more predictable, and instability associated with overinvestment in capital under common property tenure would be reduced. Also, when runs of marketable fish are reduced by natural events, the owners of the resource would still employ some fishers to remove weed fish, an activity that no one can afford to pay for under present arrangements.

Simplified Decision Making

The decision making machinery established for the United States under the Fishery Conservation and Management Act is complex and cumbersome. Criticism for the slowness with which Fishery Management Plans are prepared and revised has been strong since the FCMA was first implemented. FMPs often prove too inflexible for the timely decision making that day to day management requires. Problems with the FCMA and its complexities have been explored and explained in numerous studies. A recent one, and one which includes a good bibliography of other studies on the subject, is by Willard Barber of the University of Alaska.[3] Barber's article is based on research carried out ". . . as a 'staff member' with the North Pacific Fishery Management Council, observing and interviewing participants in the process, and reviewing literature and government documents." Barber gives excellent insights into the entire process while fitting the operations of one regional council, the North Pacific Council, into the overall picture. I recommend the entire article for a succinct evaluation of the FCMA and its history. With his permission, I have included three diagrams (Figures 14, 15 and 16) from his article that show the complexity of the process extremely well.

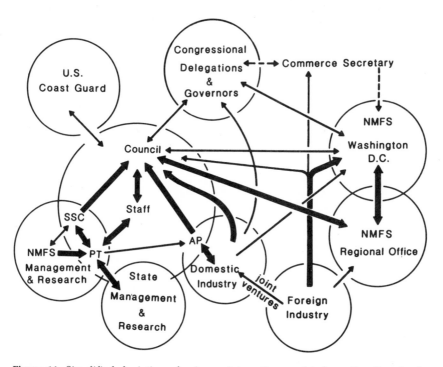

Figure 14. Simplified depiction of primary interactions and information flow in the North Pacific Fishery Management Council management process—line thickness indicates relative amount of interactions and information flow. Abbreviations are: SSC—Scientific and Statistical Committee; NMFS—National Marine Fisheries Service; PT—Plant Team; AP—Advisory Panel; State—state fisheries agencies, primarily Alaska Department of Fish and Game, but for some species Washington Department of Fisheries. (From William E. Barber, "The Fisheries Management Structure and Process Under the MFCMA: A North Pacific Perspective," *Fisheries*, 7 [6:November-December 1987], 10–17.)

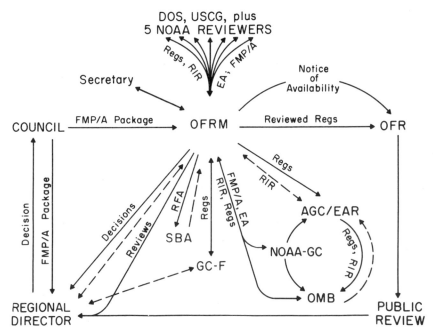

Figure 15. A synopsis of the Fisheries Management Plan or Amendment review process in Washington, D.C. Solid lines are paper flow and major communications whereas dotted lines denote conferences and verbal communications. Abbreviations are: Regs—regulations; DOS—Department of State; USCG—U.S. Coast Guard; AGC/EAR—Assistant General Council for Economic Affairs and Regulations (Department of Commerce); NOAA-GC—General Council for National Oceanographic and Atmospheric Administration; GC-F—General Council for Fisheries (NMFS); SBA—Small Business Administration, Department of Commerce; FMP/A—Fishery Management Plans and Amendments; EA—environmental assessment; RIR—Regulatory Impact Review; OFRM—Office of Fisheries Resource Management (NMFS). (From Barber, *op. cit.*, Figure 14.)

The complexities and cumbersome decision making machinery that the diagrams portray can be attributed primarily to two major underlying factors. These are: (a) the fragmentation of the United States' ocean pastures among different jurisdictions, and (b) the need to divide up (allocate) valuable fishery resources that are unowned until they are harvested. A change to full ownership with management unified for each of the separate portions of the EEZ and territorial waters of the United States would remove both the fragmentation of jurisdiction and the need to allocate fish while they are still in the ocean. Conflict would be greatly reduced, the effectiveness of management would be enhanced, and the benefits derived from the fisheries would be increased significantly.

Summary

In summary, a well planned replacement of common property tenure with full ownership of marine resources can benefit all of society with

Figure 16. Pictorial representation of the dynamic nature of fisheries management in the Magnuson Fishery Conservation Management Act as gleaned from a North Pacific experience. (From Barber, *op. cit.*, Figure 14.)

no reduction of income for anyone. Loss of income associated with reduction in fishing effort can be fully compensated from the economic rent created by the change. Once the transition to full ownership is complete, everyone will be better off. Bringing about the change will require widespread understanding of institutional arrangements governing management and use of marine fishery resources as they now exist, and of how these arrangements can be changed to the benefit of all. We do not yet know enough to say with precision how large the benefits will be, or all of the directions from which they will come. But experience with other natural resources, especially those of the field, forest, and range, assure us that full ownership is far preferable to open access or harvester rights. It will be a profound change, but one that can reward fully the effort needed to achieve it.

1   James A. Crutchfield, "Marine Resources," in Susan Hanna, *et al.*, eds., *Exploring Conflicts in the Use of the Oceans Resources,* Corvallis: Oregon Sea Grant College Program, Oregon State University, 1980, 39–53.

2   James A. Crutchfield and Giulio Pontecorvo, *The Pacific Salmon Fisheries: A Study of Irrational Conservation*, Baltimore: The Johns Hopkins University Press, 1969.

3   Willard E. Barber, "The Fisheries Management Structure and Process Under the MFCMA: A North Pacific Perspective," *Fisheries: A Bulletin of the American Fisheries Society*, 12 (November-December 1987), 10–17.

6

Pros and Cons and Interest Groups

The advantages of full ownership are enumerated and analyzed in the preceding chapters. Neither specific advantages discussed nor the overall concept of full ownership are likely to be challenged by fishery management experts. As noted in the preface, fishery resource management specialists agree that full ownership provides the most effective framework for maximizing benefits from the resources. Fisheries economists have written widely on management frameworks for fishery resources. In general works they have published on the subject, a short paragraph is almost always included in which they recognize the effectiveness of full ownership. They then dismiss this alternative as unattainable or unnecessary and move on to write at length about why one form or another of harvester rights will or will not work under certain conditions.

Despite the widespread recognition of the merit of full ownership, almost nothing has been done to explore its merit. The following quote, from the report *Conflict and Opportunity: Toward a New Policy for Canada's Pacific Fisheries*, prepared in October 1981, is indicative of attitudes toward full ownership.

> For completeness, a final alternative must be acknowledged, namely a private or public monopoly for the fishery. Certainly a single enterprise would eliminate the competitiveness among fishermen and with it the incentives to overexpand the fleet. If it were managed as a profit-maximizing company or Crown corporation, it could be expected to harvest the catch as economically as possible, to take a constructive interest in conservation and resource management and to obtain the highest return for the yield.

However, a monopoly is not to be preferred whenever there is an opportunity for a healthy competitive industry. While the Pacific fishing industry is admittedly in an unhealthy condition and urgently requires restructuring, it has not reached such an irretrievable state that it should simply be turned over to a single corporation, with all the dislocation that would entail. There are less draconian ways to improve industrial performance.[1]

The document from which the preceding quote was taken was a preliminary report of The Commission on Pacific Fisheries Policy, a commission formed in January 1981 to work out new management arrangements for Canada's Pacific fisheries. The quote is from the end of a chapter entitled "Licensing and Regulating Fleet Development." The quote includes all that the Commission's reports had to say on full ownership. The final report, published in September 1982, made no mention at all of full ownership as an option.

Although I may be accused of bias given my advocacy of full ownership, the first paragraph quoted above strikes me as fully logical and defensible, the second far less so. Mainly, I fail to see how competition among fishers can be healthy when the quantity of fish is inadequate to maintain stable prices and the harvest is carried out under the incentives of the commons. Competition among fishers to get a larger share of the harvest is at the heart of the problem. Secondly, I feel sure that less dislocation—social, economic, and political—will result from a rationally established full owner system than from the system of harvester rights that the Commission recommends, or from any other system of harvester rights.

I have read most of the literature available that discusses different measures for managing fishery resources. In doing so, I have gleaned from them arguments presented against full ownership in the short sections where it has been mentioned. These arguments are discussed in this chapter along with my conjectures as to the attitudes that different interest groups may hold toward full ownership. I also point out why I feel that most of these groups will support and help with the transition if they understand their self-interest in the issue and act accordingly.

Arguments Against Full Ownership

The body of literature focused on full ownership of fisheries, as noted above, is not large, but it is supportive of the concept. As noted in chapter 1, not much analysis is needed to see that it will work. Comments against it, however, do appear in the large body of literature that advocates various forms of harvester rights. Reasons for opposition to full ownership can be divided into three general categories: (a) ideological stances, (b) bureaucratic inefficiencies, and (c) fear of dislocation of fishing communities. Let us look at each of these separately.

94

Ideological Stances

Full ownership probably would be most effective if vested in a public agency at the national level. In market controlled, or capitalistic, economies, however, public ownership counters the basic tenet that calls for separation of political and economic systems. The size of the enterprise that I advocate is also said to contradict the capitalistic requirement for a sufficient number of enterprises to assure market control through competition, that is, to prevent monopolistic pricing. In the United States, states' rights also provide an ideological basis for opposition to unified management of marine fishery resources.

The issue of private versus public full ownership for many people is almost purely ideological; it is accepted or rejected on the basis of values, not a pragmatic assessment of the issues involved. In this case, perhaps the most telling argument for public ownership is the empirical fact that all contemporary societies have seen fit to extend public control over other natural resources. Is there a national government that does not hold substantial areas of land that are devoted primarily or solely to production of material wealth? Much of this land is forested, but public land where minerals are the most important product also is common. The most recent development in this respect is nationalization of the seabed minerals of the EEZ. Ownership of these resources in all instances remains with public agencies. Political conservatives who advocate private ownership of continental shelf lands, whether of the territorial sea or the EEZ, are few and far between; national forests have their own supporters who are sufficiently numerous and well organized to preclude privatization of national forest lands, at least in the foreseeable future. Arguments based on ideology alone are unlikely to change these resources from public to private ownership.

The arguments presented here in favor of public ownership are not based in ideology. To the contrary, my own ideological leanings favor private ownership where practical. Private ownership by corporations with shares open to purchase by all should be fully considered before settling finally on the nature of the full owner agency. For reasons given earlier and below, however, I feel that a public corporation chartered at the national level, much as private corporations are chartered by states in the United States, is preferred for fishery resources. This corporation would be charged with maximizing benefits from the marine biotic resources with full reference to market demand where possible in fulfillment of this charge. However, not all marine resources or marine resource uses lend themselves to pricing in the marketplace. Among the most important of these, or at least most difficult to price, are marine mammals maintained for essentially non-economic reasons. Recreational fishing benefits are also difficult to allocate fully through the market although room for creative development exists here. An important reason of a different nature for national control is the need for cooperation with

95

other nations to manage transboundary stocks. This need encroaches on the field of foreign relations, an area traditionally left to central governments.

The issue of monopolistic control is perhaps more practical than ideological. Monopolistic control by private interests is almost certain to lead to higher costs to consumers than where effective competition exists. The ideological issue arises with natural monopolies such as public utilities where the public is considered to be better served by a monopoly than by competitive enterprises. The logic for or against either private or public ownership of these natural monopolies is often so evenly balanced as to find both private and public ownership widely represented among them. Energy distribution enterprises provide an excellent example. Marine fishery resources can be placed in the category of natural monopolies because of the need to maximize the area of the management unit for ecological reasons. As with public utilities, they can be managed effectively under either private or public forms of ownership.

One could argue that monopolistic pricing for fisheries under private full ownership is less likely to be of concern in the United States than in countries in which the EEZ is all in one piece. The EEZ of the United States is divided irrevocably into four major and several smaller discrete parts. Giving each over to independent operation under full private ownership thus would provide a measure of competition and reduce the need for regulation against monopolistic pricing. Foreign relations aspects possibly could be handled on a fee basis by government or possibly by charter provisions. Finally, worry over monopolistic pricing can be removed completely if free trade in fish becomes the rule. If the EEZs of all countries are organized as separate entities, enterprises producing fish in the world will outnumber by far enterprises producing durable consumer goods such as automobiles and refrigerators.

In final analysis, I admit to less than total conviction that some form of private or private/public ownership would work less well than public ownership. No question exists, however, that full ownership for at least each separate part of a nation's ocean pastures is preferable to any harvester rights system. The conclusion favoring full ownership is based on the need to maintain undivided habitats. I can see no ideological or other consideration that overrides it.

Ideological issues over states' rights are countered by gains in benefits to the states that will result if ocean pastures of the United States are unified. As was brought out at the end of chapter 4, the constitutional right to divide or unify the physically separate parts of the United States' ocean pasture rests with the federal government. Coastal states are financially better off because they gained ownership of mineral resources of the seabed under territorial waters; royalties from these resources contribute to the treasuries of the coastal states. However, state control of fishery resources results in a direct financial loss to the state treasuries because of the costs of state management with no direct compensating returns. Indirect returns to coastal states through taxes on economic activities connected with fishing would be higher with the higher productivity made possible by unified management of the ocean pastures. Coastal states will benefit more from fishery resources off their coasts if they push to unify all parts of the ocean pastures under a full owner agency.

Bureaucratic Inefficiencies

Criticisms of bureaucratic inefficiencies associated with public agencies fall into two main categories: (a) a seemingly unnecessary proliferation of staff, especially within agencies that have a regulatory function and (b) a lack of response to market signals in managing resources under control of the agency. A third area, a tendency of subdivisions of the agency to take on a culture of their own that counters the interest of the organization as a whole, is also mentioned at times. This latter criticism is also characteristic of most large private enterprises so further discussion of it here seems irrelevant.

Complaints about large staffs of public agencies with regulatory functions are often heard, but what may appear to be an oversized staff is, at least in part, essential. Regulation, including regulation of who gets what (the allocation of benefits), creates an adversary relationship between those being regulated and the regulating agency. This means that a large staff must be employed by the regulator to collect and analyze information that is routinely available from enterprises in non-regulated activities whereas enterprises in regulated activities are motivated to distort information to their own benefit. The problem of distorted data prevails wherever fishing is regulated under a commons framework; examples of deliberate falsification of data on place and volume of catch are too numerous to suggest otherwise. The adverse effects on management of the warped analyses resulting from these falsified data are easily imagined.

The adversary relationship that frequently develops between fishery regulators and fishers gets in the way of data collection and analysis in another way. I recall talking with a state fishery biologist who was reassigned to work with the Pacific Fisheries Management Council, and who decried his changed relationship with fishers that resulted. He said that talking with fishers had been a delight and a chief source of information in the days before he worked with the Council. Afterward, his relationship with fishers deteriorated to the point that he made deliberate efforts to avoid them. The fishers' antagonism growing out of frustration with the Council's allocation of quotas spilled over to taint a formerly good working relationship with a fishery scientist. The loss of fishers as a source of unbiased information, and the need to rectify falsified data received from them, can be made up only by the proliferation of staff noted above as a criticism of public agencies.

Management arrangements that include any form of harvester rights will require some proliferation of staff to handle regulation connected problems as well as to process and maintain records concerning these rights. Record keeping under fishers' quotas, the rights system pushed recently as the most acceptable form of harvester rights, may prove especially costly since accurate, up-to-date records must be kept for landings of each individual rights holder. Friction between data collectors and fishers is inherent in the process. Even the most honest of fishers will fall under suspicion at times because it is so much in the interest of each fisher to underreport in order to gain additional income.

The problems growing out of regulation described above are largely eliminated by a full owner system. As with harvesters of agricultural products, fishers would be expected to follow reasonable rules when harvesting fish, but implementation of these rules would require far less record keeping than would an independent fish quota harvest rights system. Underreporting would not be a problem. Data concerning place of catch and other harvest information would be more dependable. In final analysis, a full owner system should require less proliferation of personnel than would one that employs harvester rights to control excess effort. The purpose of the full owner agency would be to produce fish, not to allocate rights to the annual quotas and then police fishers who exercise the rights under the imperatives of the commons.

The second area of concern, a lack of responsiveness to market signals in making management decisions, depends as much on the provisions of the charter of the organization as it does on who owns it. Criticism in this area of concern in the United States largely derives from the record of the Forest Service and the Bureau of Land Management in sale of timber and the leasing of grazing rights. In neither of these agencies is maximization of economic benefits clearly mandated as a major goal in the legislation under which the agencies operate. In part, this lack of legislative requirement to heed market signals results from lobbying by private forest enterprises that are in direct competition with publicly owned forests. Private forest enterprises produce under somewhat different institutional arrangements from the public agencies and claim unfair competition from the public agencies that manage forest resources. Private forest enterprises lobby to reduce this "unfair" competition. In a similar vein, users of the forests and range lands prefer that they not be required to compete in the market place for access to these resources and lobby to keep access to them below market levels. The paucity of private producers to lobby legislators in reference to marine fishery resources should simplify development of effective enabling legislation for a public full owner agency for fishery resources. In final analysis, the authorizing legislation for full owner management of fishery resources should require strong reliance on market signals and retention of ownership of fish into the marketplace. Sale through public auction probably would be the preferable way to get a majority of the fish into market channels.

Fear of Dislocation in Fishing Communities

Removal of excess fishing effort by any means will create socio-economic dislocation if only because some people will give up fishing as an occupation. A realistic response to concern over dislocation is the fact that structural and technological changes that benefit society have seldom been foregone in order to avoid occupational dislocations that they may cause. To continue overfishing and degradation of resources because too many people are fishers clearly is not in the interest of fishing communities or of society as a whole. Without question, reduction of fishing effort will take place. The question here is what measure or measures used to reduce effort will be less disruptive.

Reduction of effort under full ownership will cause far less dislocation than it will under harvester rights, and without the cost of vessel buy-back needed in the latter. Two major factors support this conclusion. First, economic rent under full ownership will accrue to the owning agency, not to individual fishers as under harvester rights. Control of the economic rent by one agency makes compensation of anyone suffering dislocation much easier than if the rent is dissipated to individual fishing enterprises. Funding of buy-back programs under harvester rights programs implemented to date has been a major problem. Vessels are not likely to be bought-back under full ownership; funds from economic rent can easily be used to compensate fully for all income lost. Secondly, a harvester rights system is likely to favor entrepreneurial ability and access to the capital needed to purchase licenses over fishing expertise. This will lead to economic concentration in fisheries which in turn encourages spatial concentration. For example, the mild form of limited entry used in Japan led to development of fishing enterprises which own multiple licenses. The owner of the fishing enterprise seldom operates the vessels to which these licenses are assigned, preferring instead to hire someone else for this task. Non-operator license holders are more likely to move the base for their vessels to large, central ports than are owner-operators. Severe social and economic dislocation took place in regional tuna fishery ports of Japan between 1949, when limited entry began, and early in the 1960s as owners relocated their base of operations to centrally located ports.[2]

Concentration of ownership of harvester rights may be judged desirable or undesirable depending on the standpoint of the observer, but it does mean that owner-operator vessel owners will decrease in number with consequent effects on the socio-economic structure of fishing communities. Those who consider concentration to be undesirable may suggest that harvester rights ownership be controlled through legislation, but to do so has proved difficult. Also, a full ownership agency, as noted earlier, will be far more likely to engage fishers in weeding operations than will the managing agency under a harvester rights system. The overall reduction in numbers of people actually engaged in fishing, that is in removal of both commercial and trash species from the ocean, will be smaller under a full owner than under a harvester rights system.

Anticipated Reaction to Full Ownership

Summary rejection is usually the initial reaction to any change as profound as full ownership tenure would be for marine fishery resources. To understand the benefits of full ownership well enough to accept the change requires the integration of fairly complex factors in a broad framework. This requires time. With understanding, however, acceptance should come easily for a vast majority of the population. The probable reaction of various interest groups as they move toward acceptance can be anticipated as follows.

Consumers and Taxpayers

Initial reaction from consumers and taxpayers is likely to be slight. Fishery resources, as is brought out in the preface, directly affect only a small part of a nation's population to the extent that they are encouraged to master the complexities of, and work to improve, fishery resources management. I believe, however, that opportunities foregone in marine fishery resources management are of sufficient magnitude to create interest among most consumers and taxpayers. Needless waste and costs to taxpayers such as those which exist in fisheries at present also often create interest out of proportion to the direct effect that they have on individual citizens once the public becomes aware of them. Public discussion of issues of this nature increases public interest. Public support for a change to full ownership will grow over time if it becomes a topic of expanded debate in fishery and legislative circles.

Fishing Communities

Adverse reaction can be expected initially in fishing communities, but assurance of equitable treatment during the transition should lead to fairly rapid acceptance. No one knows better than fishers the adverse effects that excess fishing effort has had since the 1960s. Decreased catch rates, smaller fish, longer trips, more crowded fishing grounds, and increased competition for docking space have become part and parcel of fishing as an occupation. Commercial fishers have a gut level understanding of the underlying causes for these worrisome features that have come to be associated with fishing since the tragedy of the commons set in. The implications of opportunity costs have been driven home to them through the precipitous rise in the real value of fish that created the adverse effects of too much fishing effort. More fishers work as hard, make longer trips, catch fewer fish, and end up making ends meet no better nor worse on average than they did when fish prices were low.

In my experience, fishers are an independent and fair minded occupational group, and all, or at least the vast majority, lament the degradation of resources that has come with excess fishing effort. They have resisted development of harvester rights because of the inequities involved, the proliferation of regulations and controls that must accompany such rights, and an uneasiness that goes with the fear of being forced out of fishing with nothing in return except the possible sale of their vessel to a publicly funded buy-back agency. The opportunity to see stocks restored, catch rates go up, incomes remain at an assured level during transition, and freedom to remain as fishers unfettered by controls on vessel characteristics and fishing methods designed to reduce their efficiency, or to withdraw with assurance of full compensation for fishery related income given up, should result in general acceptance among fishers once the newness of the idea is replaced with full understanding of it.

Buyers and Processors

Dependence on auctions for purchase of fish may be upsetting to buyers and processors who have assured themselves supplies of fish by forming close working relationships with fishers through financial or other ties. Assurance of larger and more regular supplies of good quality fish, however, should lead to fairly ready acceptance by this group as a whole. Their businesses run more smoothly and profitably if they can provide customers a good quality product consistently on a year round basis. For example, when asked why he served Norwegian salmon when he could have had Washington salmon, a Los Angeles restaurant owner replied that Norwegian salmon was the only fish he could depend upon for consistent quality.[3]

Fishery Resource Managers

Fishery resource managers include present federal and state employees—biologists, economists, data collection and processing specialists, wardens and the like—who now look after fishery resources. Job uncertainties associated with reorganization of the existing fishery resources management system will create uneasiness among this group, especially among state employees. However, more investment in fishery resource management is needed, not less. Funds to support expanded investment will be available under full ownership. All existing positions involved with fishery resources management in state and federal agencies can be integrated into the full ownership agency to the advantage of that agency. Present employees can, in most instances, be retained profitably in the geographic area as well as in the occupation in which they now work. Opportunities for advancement typical of expanding enterprises will be high; regulatory tasks that create distasteful friction with harvesters will decrease. Job satisfaction will be much higher for most employees of a full owner agency than for employees in the existing system. If some people do lose their position against their will, they can be compensated for losses incurred. Fishery resource managers can be expected to support full ownership if the transition is handled properly.

Legislators

Strong adverse reaction from legislators, especially state legislators, with fishery oriented constituencies can be expected initially. Also, state legislators as a whole traditionally have delegated authority for marine fisheries management with extreme reluctance. Most have continued to maintain full control, or at least control over major aspects of fisheries, despite general recognition of the need for far more flexible arrangements. To ask them to give up control completely to the federal level will arouse issues of states' rights, of the need for local control, of the potential for corruption of big bureaucracy by special interest groups, or whatever else can be dredged up as an excuse to resist the idea.[4]

Fishery resources, however, are different from the mineral resources that were the main issue in the scramble for resources underlying the Submerged Lands Act. Mineral resources, primarily oil, covered by the Submerged Lands Act are now owned outright by the coastal state concerned. Royalties from oil brings in far more income per barrel to the state treasury than do taxes from comparable privately owned terrestrial resources within that state. Constituencies of legislators thus find it in their self-interest to support legislators who work for state ownership of continental shelf mineral resources. The opposite is true for fishery resources. Fragmentation of ocean pastures that goes with state control reduces benefits to the constituents of coastal state legislators from fishery resources. Increased landings of fish from better management under unified control will benefit constituents. Once constituencies realize where their self-interest lies, support from coastal state legislators should be forthcoming.

Federal legislators from coastal states can be expected in the beginning to side with state legislators of the states they represent. However, as national representatives with national responsibilities, their opposition should wane sooner than will that of state legislators. Federal and state legislators from inland states will support the concept from early on since they personally have nothing to lose in the way of control over resources, and their constituents have much to gain.

Recreational Fishers

The position of recreational fishers is somewhat difficult to predict. Few states now require purchases of licenses or payment in any form that contributes to the costs of management of marine fishery resources. Giving up a free ride is seldom easy. However, pressure for a monetary contribution from recreational fishers has increased since the tragedy of the commons set in and created the need for marine fishery resources management. Advocates have appeared for both state and federal licenses and, with user fees gaining acceptance in principle for many other outdoor recreational activities, recreational fishers are likely to begin making a contribution soon whatever the institutional arrangements. Recreational fishers will benefit greatly from increased catches as stocks are restored. This prospect should be the ultimate one that convinces recreational fishers of the advantage of full ownership.

In summary, losers through a change to full ownership are far outnumbered by winners. Petroleum companies will suffer some loss because the amount of fuel used in fishing will decrease. Boat builders and other businesses that support the fishing fleet will lose somewhat, but as noted earlier, provision can be made to compensate them for losses directly related to the change to full ownership. As catch rates increase, expanded recreational fishing will create business for this group. Legislative assistants who are primarily engaged in hearings on fisheries and other activities connected with development of legislation may find time on their hands and a need to acquire new expertise. Directors and staff of organizations of commercial fishers also are likely to find work loads reduced as lobbying efforts to increase allocations of resources to members are no longer needed. However, the numbers here are small; the individuals concerned are usually energetic and adaptable. First choice on new positions in the full owner agencies can be offered to all persons in these categories in order to meet fully the criterion that no one be adversely affected by the change to institutional arrangements based on full ownership. Societies do not often have an opportunity to make a change that hurts no one and leaves most people better off. Passing up one of this magnitude is difficult to justify.

1   The Commission on Pacific Fisheries Policy, *Conflict and Opportunity—Toward a New Policy for Canada's Pacific Fisheries: A Preliminary Report*, Vancouver, British Columbia: Department of Fisheries and Oceans, 1981:35. The final report of the Commission is entitled *Turning the Tide—A New Policy for Canada's Pacific Fisheries*. The Commission was headed by Peter H. Pearse, a professor of economics at the University of British Columbia who has a strong interest in fisheries economics.

2   E. A Keen, "Regional Concentration of the Japanese Tuna Fishery," *Yearbook of the Association of Pacific Coast Geographers*, 31 (1971), 127–140 *passim*.

3   John L. Pitts, "Opinion," *Pacific Fishing*, 9 (February 1988):66.

4   The reluctance of the California Legislature to delegate day to day control of the state's fishery to the California Department of Fish and Game is fairly typical of the attitude of many state legislatures. As one commentator pointed out, the State Fish and Game Code established by the legislature ". . . requires scientific evidence of 'danger of irreparable injury' to a resource before the Department has any management authority." He concluded that "Until the legislature no longer has the last word on anything but clearly stated and publicly agreed upon guidelines, California's natural resources will continue to suffer from political management that satisfies no one for long." Carl Nettleton, "DFG Doesn't Have Authority It Needs," *Western Outdoor News*, 22 January 1988, 7.

7

Recap and Reiteration Through Example

The purchase of Alaska by the United States in 1867 included the Pribilof Islands, the breeding grounds for the world's largest herd of fur seals. The herd probably was close to its natural limits in size at the time of purchase with an estimated population in excess of two million. Congress passed an act in 1870 providing for the management of the seals, and a lease was let in 1870 to the Alaskan Commercial Company of San Francisco to harvest up to 100,000 seals annually under specified conditions. All harvest was to be on land as it had been when under Russian control. The company harvested approximately two million seal skins, the maximum number permitted, during its 20 year lease. A new lease was signed with a different company in 1890, but only 300,000 skins were harvested during its 20 year term.

Overexploitation, not the change in companies, accounted for the decrease in harvest during the period of the second lease. Fur seals had become a very valuable commodity by the 1870s; steam powered vessels and other technological developments soon made it possible to harvest them on the high seas. The annual migration of the seals takes them to waters off southern California in the eastern Pacific and to waters off southern Japan in the western Pacific. Pelagic sealing, as the practice of high seas harvest during these migrations came to be known, developed rapidly. The pelagic harvest, participated in by Canadian, Russian, Japanese, and United States vessels, peaked at about 62,000 skins in 1894. A majority of these came from the Pribilof herds, the remainder from herds that breed on the Russian owned Commander Islands in the western part of the Bering Sea. The pelagic harvest exceeded the land based harvest during the 1890s; the total harvest fell steadily. By 1910, the population of the Pribilof herds had fallen to about one-tenth of its size in 1870.

105

North Pacific fur seal management created an international controversy in the 1890s comparable to the controversy over international whaling in recent years. The United States claimed exclusive control over the Pribilof Island seals and seized several sealing vessels operating near it in the late 1880s. Various agreements worked out between the United States and Great Britain, which handled Canadian international relations at the time, early in the 1890s culminated in fairly stringent controls on vessels registered in the two countries. Not unexpectedly, United States and Canadian citizens changed the country of registry of their sealing vessels and continued to participate without controls. Japanese and Russian vessels continued pelagic harvests unregulated. The harvest of all countries declined by the end of the century to a point that demonstrated the mechanics of the tragedy of the commons about as fully as it can be demonstrated. All realized that much could be gained and little or nothing lost through cooperation. A mutual willingness to negotiate resulted.

The international controversy over seals terminated with the Fur Seal Treaty of 1911 among the four nations whose citizens engaged in harvest of the seals—the United States, Canada, Japan, and Russia. The treaty has continued with more or less its original provisions except for a brief lapse during World War II. For any treaty to continue despite the great changes within and among these four nations suggests that it has much to offer. This one does. It moved the seal resources out of common tenure and under a full owner system. Its record is one that demonstrates the effect that this change can have both on the total harvest and on the costs of harvest. One may question the 15/15/70 division of the final profits as provided in the treaty, but no one can question that each nation gets more than it did from the paltry harvests in the years leading up to the treaty.

Harvest First, Divide Afterward

The signatories of the treaty in essence said, "Let us harvest the seals in a way that maximizes benefits from the resource, and then divide these benefits equitably among us." The nature of the resource clearly pointed out the best way to do this. All seals return to the aforementioned Pribilof and Commander islands of the Bearing Sea and haul out on land for the mating season. Dominant bulls form harems of a dozen or more females; males that lose out in the mating game, or that have not yet entered it, end up in a separate group apart from the breeding herd. A more mobile creature than a seal in the ocean is hard to imagine; a less mobile one on land is equally so. These "surplus" males are easily killed with clubs wielded by hand (Figure 17). Their skins are then removed immediately and their carcasses processed for animal food. No seals are lost during the harvest; the size of the next crop is unaffected. The National Marine Fisheries Service now handles the harvest of the Pribilof Island herd. In 1977, it paid $273,000 for the harvest and processing of

The drive in waiting.   Sealers knocking down a "pou."   Natives skinning.

THE FUR-SEAL INDUSTRY OF THE PRIBYLOV ISLANDS, ALASKA.

Figure 17. Harvesting fur seals on the Pribilof Islands. This figure was drawn a few years after the United States purchased Alaska. A picture of the harvest today would be different only in the style of clothing worn by the harvesters. Improvements on the technology and methods of harvest would be difficult to imagine. (From Goode, *op. cit.*, note 2, chapter 3.)

seals and their skins. It sold the harvest for $1,617,225, or almost six times the cost of taking and processing it. Under terms of the treaty, 15 percent of the income from the harvest went to Canada, 15 percent to Japan, and the United States kept 70 percent. The USSR harvested the Commander Island crop under similar arrangements, again with Canada and Japan each receiving fifteen percent of the income.

The harvest at sea, the pelagic harvest, was incredibly wasteful by comparison. Seals had to be located in the open ocean and captured with harpoons; a far more costly process than harvest on land. Seals were lost when they wriggled free from harpoons—many died of their wounds—or fell off the harpoon after dying but before they could be hauled aboard. Skins were damaged in the harpooning process. Most carcasses went overboard once the skins were removed because processing the small numbers taken by each vessel for animal food or other uses was not worthwhile. Distinction between males and females was difficult even if the sealers had desired to make such a distinction. This, and the incentives of the commons to maximize returns from each trip, led to severe decimation of the herds.

As is always the case under the commons, the fur seal harvest costs tended to equal total value of the harvest, and because the harvest on land already equalled the maximum sustainable yield, decimation of the herds commenced when pelagic sealing began. Had the fur seals remained under common tenure, they surely would have followed their

107

former coinhabitants of the North Pacific, the Steller's sea cows, to extinction. The population of fur seals dropped from between two and three million to between two and three hundred thousand between 1870 and 1910. The law of supply clearly had gone into reverse under the open access of common property tenure.

Rational management of the fur seals under full ownership began in 1911. The standing population of the Pribilof herd at present averages about 1.4 million, about five times that of 1910. It probably will not reach its former size again because of human competition for food through increased fishing in the area, and because of the loss of seals that become entangled in monofilament nets lost or abandoned in the ocean by fishers. This base population, if slightly smaller than in 1870, produces far more benefits for the citizens of the three nations concerned than possibly could be expected from harvest on the high seas. The same holds true for the Commander Island herd. Is it any wonder that the treaty has survived the trials associated with the enormous changes within and among these four nations?

The four signatory nations of the Fur Seal Treaty managed to establish *de facto* ownership of the seal herds much as the United States and Canada established *de facto* ownership of the Pacific halibut between 1923 and the late 1950s. The main difference between the two examples is the extent to which the owning nations exercised control. The annual halibut quota is divided before harvest with the consequent reduction of benefits noted earlier. The potential ratio of rent to harvest costs that could have been collected through efficient harvest probably exceeds the nearly six to one ratio noted for fur seals. All rent potential is dissipated in the cost of the pre-allocated harvest, the conduct of which also reduces the overall value of the harvest. Ownership of the products of the fur seal, on the other hand, is retained into the marketplace by the owner. The results are profoundly different. But the fact that they are so different is scarcely astounding. The difference is what one would expect from changing to full ownership after the tragedy point in exploitation of a resource is reached.

The 1982 Law of the Sea Treaty gives nations much firmer rights to fishery resources off their coasts than existed for either seals or halibut in the North Pacific. All major stocks and their habitats except stocks of the highly migratory species such as tuna, billfishes, and whales can be brought under national control. To extend national control into a full ownership arrangement with ownership retained into the marketplace would be more effective for fishery resources than it was for seal resources. Full ownership would exist for the national ocean pastures and all stocks within them; the seals were owned on a species basis only. Establishing full ownership clearly is in the interest of all concerned.

Recap

"The time has come," the walrus said, "to speak of many things." In reference to the management of marine fishery resources, the things to talk about center on the nature of ownership and the size of the ownership unit. The law of supply served us well as long as nature's bounty met or exceeded our needs. Demand rose constantly through the ages as population grew and techniques for harvest and delivery of fish and shellfish improved. Large increases in demand were met with matching increases in production but brought very small upward movement in price even if harvest technology remained constant. With the new techniques and tools made possible by the Industrial Revolution, the costs of production decreased markedly. The law of supply worked as it should. Lower production costs brought lower prices, and lower prices brought increased consumption. Fishers increased production of fish as long as fish stocks supported the increased catches. Technological improvements in fishing methods and growth in demand for fish led to an explosion of fishing effort as the world recovered from World War II. Fishing pressure grew on stock after stock of fish in more or less direct proportion to the market value of the species. Excessive fishing effort began to push exploitation of the more valuable stocks beyond the tragedy point with increasing rapidity from the mid-1960s.

The law of supply works in reverse under common tenure once nature's bounty no longer suffices. When the tragedy point is reached, supply at best becomes fixed since the imperatives of the commons work against investment to increase productivity of the resources. Continued growth in demand does signal fishers to increase their effort, to try to catch more fish in response to the higher prices they receive for their catches. But supply falls as effort increases. Every increase in demand brings a further decrease in landings as rising prices keep fishers' incomes more or less constant and fishing effort high even though fewer fish are caught.

The law of supply can be made to work in our favor again by doing with fishery resources what was done with common tenure in other renewable natural resources—getting rid of it. Common tenure gives the wrong signals after the tragedy point is reached and causes us to overtax nature's bounty. Full ownership gives the right signals; it provides incentives to invest to help nature produce more of what we want. Rights to harvest, on the other hand, continue to provide the same signals as common tenure; they only provide incentives to invest in the means to harvest, not the means to make the resource produce more.

History proves that full ownership works best for all natural resources once the tragedy point is reached. Full ownership itself, however, can take a number of forms. The characteristics of a natural resource weigh heavily in the determination of the most productive form of full ownership for it. With agriculture, where the original biotic community is largely obliterated, the family owned farm works best in most instances. Constant attention is needed if the plants and animals that are chosen to replace the original community are to be properly husbanded and helped to produce effectively. Emergency situations such as broken fences, sick cows, and floods often require special effort at odd hours of the day or night. Wage workers have less incentive to do this than does a full owner or members of his family.

With fisheries, working to keep the original biotic community essentially intact pays high rewards. Under common tenure, we remove the most desirable species which helps the less desirable species expand. Reversal of this incentive is a major first step in working with the ecosystem to help the desired species compete to maintain their niche in the system. Full ownership gives the incentives needed to work with the ecosystem as a whole in order to help the desired species maintain or expand their niche in the food web. Given the nature of the marine ecosystem and of the overlapping habitats of the desired species, the scale of the ownership unit, not the need for constant husbandry of domesticated species as with agriculture, becomes the dominant characteristic determining the nature of the preferred ownership agency. The minimum size of the optimum management unit becomes each separate part of a nation's ocean pastures after the compromises growing out of the need for supporting legal systems are made. Further division of area or sharing of jurisdiction with lower levels of government can only be counterproductive.

The only major point remaining in question for me is the nature of the full owner agency. I lean toward a public corporation under national control, but private or private/public corporations may work better in some instances, a national level public agency such as the United States established for managing marine minerals in its EEZ in others. For example, possibly the best arrangement for the Canadian Atlantic Ocean pasture, with its large fisheries-dependent population, would be a single private or quasi-private corporation, shares of which would be held by fishery households. For the Pacific Ocean pastures of the United States and of Canada, where commercial fishers make up a small part of the total population and recreational fishers are numerous, a public corporation may prove to be the preferred arrangement. Whatever its form of ownership, however, a country and its citizens can only be better off if the entire production and marketing process is carried out by a full owner agency.

People did get hurt in the transition from common to full ownership tenure for other renewable natural resources. Reams have been written about the economic hardships and inequities brought about by the enclosure of common lands in England and Wales. Hollywood has made the friction between the cattle ranchers and sheepherders, between livestock owners and squatters, over range lands open for common use a well known part of American folklore. The friction and suffering were real; the transition is still incomplete for grazing lands held by federal agencies

110

in the United States. The tragedy point was reached for these resources in the 1880s. It took over a half century to get the Taylor Grazing Act through Congress and bring a semblance of management to these resources. Harvester rights still get in the way of management of public range lands and keep productivity at lower levels than it would be under full ownership. At present, we are following the same muddling, wasteful course in marine resources. This need not be so.

A change in institutional arrangements to include full ownership is a conservative response. Such ownership works with other natural resources, and it can work with marine fishery resources as well. Once this fact is understood by the public at large, legislation to establish full ownership should follow more or less as a matter of course. Design of the full owner agency will require considerable time and effort. It should involve the best talents available on public and business administration as well as on fisheries management. Public discussion should be extended and involve the nation in its entirety. The end result can and should be a framework that runs smoothly, effectively, and with little need for intervention from government. Fishery resource managers will be able to devote their full time to maintaining a healthy and productive resource, not to resolving arguments over who gets the benefits from them. Commercial fishers will be able to operate with no more rules and regulations than are imposed upon the grain harvesters mentioned earlier. Recreational fishers will be able to catch more fish of the species that they desire. Consumers will have more and better fish, and taxpayers will be relieved of the burden of supporting fisheries. Can anyone doubt that it is in the interest of everyone—fishers and non-fishers, coastal residents and inland residents alike—to press for full ownership of unified ocean pastures?

Glossary

Anadromous fish: Species of fish that spawn in fresh water but mature in the ocean, such as striped bass and salmon.

By-catch: Fish caught unintentionally while fishing for other species. Also, incidental catch.

Common property resource: A natural resource open to harvest by anyone without restriction. Synonymous with open access resource. As used here, a resource which yields no economic rent (see below).

Economic rent: Any payment to an owner of a productive resource that is an amount in excess of the payment needed to keep the resource in its current use. Applied to fisheries, the amount of pure profit that can be gained from a fishery resource by using no more fishing effort than needed to harvest the resource. Under open access, the resource would yield no economic rent, whereas a sole owner would seek to maximize economic rent.

EEZ: Exclusive economic zone (see below).

Exclusionary right: As used here, the right to exclude anyone from use of (access to) a natural resource.

Exclusive economic zone: Loosely, the area of marine waters within 200 nautical miles of a nation's coasts over which it has the right to control use of natural resources. More specifically, the area between the boundary of a nation's territorial seas and a line 200 nautical miles from its coasts over which it has rights to control use of natural resources but has no control over other uses. Under certain circumstances, the 1982 Law of the Sea Treaty permits extension of control of resources beyond 200 nautical miles. The EEZ of the United States extends from 3 to 200 nautical miles.

Ex-vessel price: Price paid to fishermen for fish.

FAO: Food and Agricultural Organization of the United Nations.

FCMA: Fishery Conservation and Management Act (see below).

Fishery Conservation and Management Act: The basic federal law governing management of marine fisheries in the United States. Passed in 1976 and amended several times since, this act is administered through the Department of Commerce. The act subsequently was renamed the Magnuson Fishery Conservation and Management Act in honor of its main sponsor, Senator Warren Magnuson of the State of Washington.

Fishery Conservation Zone: Zone of federal control of United States' fisheries between territorial waters and a distance of 200 nautical miles as defined in the FCMA.

Fishery Management Council: A fisheries management body established by the FCMA to manage fishery resources in designated regions of the United States. Membership varies in size depending on the number of states involved. Eight regional councils exist.

Fishery Management Plan: A document prepared under supervision of the appropriate Fishery Management Council or councils for management of stocks of fish judged to be in need of management. The Secretary of Commerce must approve FMPs.

FMP: Fishery Management Plan (see above).

Harvester rights: Rights to harvest a natural resource given to a limited number of individuals or firms. The holder of the rights gains ownership to specific products of the resource, for example, of individual fish, with harvest of the products. Harvester rights in fisheries result in economic rent from the fisheries which, under present arrangements, goes to the harvester.

Highly migratory species: Marine species whose life cycle includes lengthy migrations, usually through the EEZ of two or more countries as well as into international waters.

Law of supply: The quantity supplied of a good or service varies directly with its price; the lower the price the smaller the quantity supplied, and the higher the price the larger the quantity supplied.

Limited access: As used in fisheries, usually the same as harvester rights (see above) but sometimes used to include all controlled access to use of a natural resource, including full ownership. Also, limited entry.

Limited entry: See limited access above.

MFCMA: Magnuson Fishery Conservation and Management Act. Same as FCMA.

MSY: Maximum sustainable yield. The maximum yield that can be expected from a natural resource over time through the management of the resource. Recognized as an impractical goal in fisheries because of variations in productivity caused by natural factors beyond control of humans, MSY is nevertheless a concept used frequently in discussions about fishery resources management.

NMFS: National Marine Fisheries Service. The main federal agency of the United States for marine fisheries. The NMFS is subordinate to the National Oceanographic and Atmospheric Administration of the Department of Commerce.

OMB: Office of Management and Budget. Main budgetary agency for the Executive Branch of the government of the United States.

Open access resource: See common property resource above.

Opportunity cost: The most favorable price that can be expected for use of an asset or assets.

Optimum yield: As defined by the FCMA, the amount of fish (a) which will provide the greatest overall benefit to the nation with special reference to food production and recreational opportunities, and (b) which is prescribed as such on the basis of the MSY from such fishery, as modified by any relevant economic, social, or ecological factor.

Population: In a fisheries management sense, all the individuals of a given species inhabiting a specified region. A population can be divided into subpopulations, which are self-sustaining genetic units.

Stock: A group of fish which can be exploited and managed independently.

Territorial waters: The area beyond the tidal base line of the open coasts of a country over which that country exercises full control except for innocent passage of foreign vessels. Set at a maximum of 12 nautical miles in breadth by the 1982 Law of the Sea Treaty, the United States claims territorial waters three nautical miles in width.

Tragedy of the commons: The degradation of a common property natural resource through continued exploitation of that resource after the MSY has been reached. If the resource is sufficiently valuable and no controls on exploitation are imposed, the resource may be exploited to extinction.

Transboundary stocks: Stocks of fish that migrate across international boundaries or, in the case of the United States, across the boundaries between states or Fishery Management Council areas of control.

Weed fish: A species of fish that interferes with harvest of other species and that reduces the production of desired species through competition within the marine biotic community. Includes so-called trash fish, species that are caught incidentally along with target species but are of insufficient value to justify retention for market.

Suggested Readings

Abgall, J. "Fishing Industry: In Support of a Single Manager." *Canadian Journal of Agricultural Economics*, 26 (1978), 35–42.

Adasiak, A. "Alaska's New Experience with Limited Entry." *Journal of the Fisheries Research Board of Canada*, 33 (1979), 770–782.

Anderson, Lee G. *The Economics of Fisheries Management*. Baltimore: The Johns Hopkins University Press, 1986.

Beddington, J. R., and R. Bruce Rettig. *Approaches to the Regulation of Fishing Effort*. Fishery Technical Paper 243, Food and Agricultural Organization of the United Nations, 1984.

Crutchfield, James A., ed. *Biological and Economic Aspects of Fisheries Management*. Seattle: University of Washington Press, 1959.

Crutchfield, James A., and Giulio Pontecorvo. *The Pacific Salmon Fishery: A Study in Irrational Conservation*. Baltimore: The Johns Hopkins University Press, 1969.

Dewar, Margaret E. *Industry in Trouble: The Federal Government and New England Fisheries*. Philadelphia: Temple University Press, 1983.

Ellis, Derek V., ed. *Pacific Salmon Management for People*. Geographic Series, 13. Victoria: University of Victoria, 1977.

Farnell, John, and James Elles. *In Search of a Common Fishing Policy*. Aldershot, England: Gower Publishing Company, 1984.

Gulland, J. A. "World Resources of Fisheries and Their Management," pp. 841–1090 in Otto Kinne, ed., *Marine Ecology* V, Part 2. New York: John Wiley and Sons, 1983.

Hoskins, W. G., and L. Dudley Stamp. *The Common Lands of England and Wales*. London: Collins, 1963.

Jackson, Roy I., and William D. Royce. *An Interpretive History of the International North Pacific Fisheries Commission*. London: Fishing News Books, 1986.

Keen, E. A. "Limited Entry: The Case of the Japanese Tuna Fishery," pp. 146–158 in Adam Sokoloski, ed., *Ocean Fishery Management: Discussions and Research*. Department of Commerce, NOAA Technical Report NMFS Circ-371, 1972.

Libecap, Gary D. *Locking Up the Range—Federal Land Controls and Grazing*. Cambridge: Ballinger, 1981.

McEvoy, Arthur E. *The Fisherman's Problem: Ecology and Law in the California Fisheries, 1850–1980*. New York: Cambridge University Press, 1986.

Mead, W. J. "Log Sales vs. Timber Sales," in William McKillop and Walter J. Mead, eds., *Timber Policy Issues in British Columbia*. Vancouver: University of British Columbia Press, 1976.

Miles, Edward, Robert Pealy, and Robert Stokes, eds. *Natural Resources Economics and Policy Applications: Essays in Honor of James A. Crutchfield*. Seattle: University of Washington Press, 1986.

Norton, V., T. Smith, and I. Strand, eds. *Stripers*. Maryland Sea Grant Program, University of Maryland, 1984.

Rettig, R. Bruce. "Practices and Problems with License Limitation in the USA and Canada," pp. 251–273 in *Expert Consultation on the Regulation of Fishing Effort*. Food and Agricultural Organization Fisheries Report Number 289, Supplement 3, 1985.

Roppel, Alton Y. *Management of Northern Fur Seals on the Pribilof Islands, Alaska*. Washington: Department of Commerce, NOAA Technical Report NMFS 4, 1984.

Seidman, Harold, and Robert Gilmour. *Politics, Position, and Power: From the Positive to the Regulatory State*. New York: Oxford University Press, 1986, 4th ed.

Tate, W.E. *The English Village Community and the Enclosure Movement*. London: Victor Gollancy, Ltd., 1967.

U. S. Forest Service. *An Assessment of the Forest and Rangeland Situation in the United States, Forest Resource Report 22*. Washington: Government Printing Office, 1981.

Waugh, Geoffrey. *Fisheries Management: Theoretical Developments and Contemporary Applications.* Boulder: Westview Press, 1984.

Weeks, E. P., and L. Mazany. *The Future of Atlantic Fisheries.* Montreal: The Institute for Research on Public Policy, 1983.

Wise, Mark. *The Common Fisheries Policy of the European Community.* London: Methuen, 1984.

Selected Agencies Concerned With Marine Fisheries

Federal Government

National Marine Fisheries Service
1825 Connecticut Avenue,NW
Washington, DC 20235

U.S. Fish and Wildlife Service
18th and C Streets, NW
Washington, DC 20240

Regional Fisheries Management Councils

Caribbean Fishery Management Council
Banco de Ponce Building, Suite 1108
Hato Rey, Puerto Rico 00918

Gulf of Mexico Fishery Management Council
5401 West Kennedy Boulevard, Suite 881
Tampa, FL 33609

Mid-Atlantic Fishery Management Council
Federal Building, Room 2115
North and News Streets
Dover, DE 19901

New England Fishery Management Council
5 Broadway (Route 1)
Saugus, MA 01906

North Pacific Fishery Management Council
411 West 4th Avenue, Suite 2d
Post Office Box 103136
Anchorage, AK 99510

Pacific Fishery Management Council
Metro Center, Suite 420
2000 Southwest First Avenue
Portland, OR 97201

South Atlantic Fishery Management Council
Southpark Building, Suite 306
1 Southpark Circle
Charleston, SC 29407

Western Pacific Fishery Management Council
1164 Bishop Street, Room 1405
Honolulu, HI 96813

Regional Fisheries Commissions

Atlantic States Marine Fisheries Commission
1717 Massachusetts Avenue, NW
Washington, DC 20036

Gulf States Marine Fisheries Commission
P.O. Box 726
Ocean Springs, MS 39564

Pacific Marine Fisheries Commission
1400 Southwest 5th Avenue, Room 305
Portland, OR 97201

Non-governmental Agencies

National Fisheries Institute
2000 M Street, NW, Suite 580
Washington, DC 20036

Sport Fishing Institute
1010 Massachusetts Avenue, NW, Suite 100
Washington, DC 20001